The misuse of heroin is on the increase. In 1955 Britain had 54 registered addicts, in 1983 the figure of 5,000 was almost 50 per cent up on 1982. Today, government estimates suggest there are as many as 60,000 addicts and perhaps as many as another 60,000 occasional users.

Tom Field is an ex-heroin addict and *Escaping the Dragon* was written to provide immediate information for parents, family, friends, teachers, health professionals and addicts themselves, about the misuse of heroin, the physical and psychological addiction, the consequences and social effects, and help required.

The themes and issues in *Escaping the Dragon* are based on the author's own experience and research, but they are pertinent to anyone concerned about, interested in or actively combating the problem of heroin addiction.

ESCAPING THE DRAGON

ESCAPING THE DRAGON

TOM FIELD

London
UNWIN PAPERBACKS
Boston   Sydney

First published in Great Britain by Unwin Paperbacks 1985

UNWIN ® PAPERBACKS
40 Museum Street, London WCIA 1LU, UK

Unwin Paperbacks
Park Lane, Hemel Hempstead, Herts HP2 4TE, UK

George Allen & Unwin Australia Pty Ltd
8 Napier Street, North Sydney, NSW 2060, Australia

Unwin Paperbacks with the
Port Nicholson Press
PO Box 11-838 Wellington, New Zealand

ISBN 0 04 613062 4

Set in 11 on 13 point Sabon
by V & M Graphics Ltd, Aylesbury Bucks
and printed in Great Britain by
The Guernsey Press Co Ltd, Guernsey, Channel Islands.

Contents

Author's note	*page* xi
Chapter One Introduction	1
Chapter Two – Availability	8
Production	9
Importation	12
Dealing	15
What can be done	21
Chapter Three – Willingness	24
Barriers	26
Weakness	30
Chance	34
Building barriers	39
Chapter Four – Heroin	42
Physical effects	45
Psychological effects	50
Towards addiction	53
Chapter Five – Addiction	59
Deprivation	61
Disintegration	64
Money	70
Trying to stop	74
Chapter Six – Recognition	78
Objects	79
Physical Appearances	83
Behaviour	85

Chapter Seven – Help   91
    First steps   94
    Professional Help   96
    Alternatives   100
    Continuing Support   105
Glossary   109
Appendix   111

To my family

Author's Note

I have used the term 'addiction' to refer exclusively to physical addiction, unless otherwise qualified. Similarly, an 'addict' is someone who has a physical addiction. The term 'heroin user' refers to anyone who takes heroin, whether addicted or not. Whenever I have used a pronoun to replace a noun that could be of either sex, such as 'addict', I have used the masculine pronoun. This is done only for convenience. It should not be taken to imply, for example, that all addicts are male, although, in fact, there are considerably more male than female addicts.

CHAPTER ONE

Introduction

'It's a shattering experience to discover that both your children are heroin addicts. You can't help feeling a failure, and so bewildered. You don't know where you went wrong and you don't know where to turn for help. It's not knowing the first thing about it that is so terrifying.'

Those are the words of a father. Not just any father. Mine. There is no way in which I or my brother, whose contribution to this book amounts to co-authorship, can change what we put our parents through. Perhaps, however, we can put at the disposal of other parents the sort of information that should have been, but was not, available to ours. Instead, they were forced to find a path through the frequently conflicting advice of the 'experts' by trial and error. Because we were a little ahead of some of our friends in becoming addicted, our parents found that *they* were being asked for advice: the tiny amount of knowledge they had acquired was already precious.

This book, then, is primarily addressed to parents. Most believe it could not happen to their children; they do not know how to recognise the signs that it is happening; and they do not know what to do about it. It is so easy to shut your eyes to the fact that something is wrong, so easy to let ignorance convince you that you must be mistaken. This is particularly true if you consider your children to be well-adjusted, 'normal'.

One of the misconceptions about heroin is that no one who is 'normal' could possibly take it, let alone become addicted to it. In other words, that heroin taking is only a symptom of delinquency. Certainly, it is almost always symptomatic of some other 'problem', but so often these 'problems' are not the problems of delinquency but the problems of everyday life to which everyone is subject.

What determines whether someone will try heroin is, firstly, its availability: if many of one's friends are taking it, for example, one is much more likely to try it. Its availability is ensured by the enormous profits it generates. These in turn depend upon the demand for the drug, which grows as more people try it. Heroin, to a large extent, creates its own market. Of course, that it is there is not enough: one has to be willing to try it. This willingness can be temporary, a moment of weakness, boredom or carelessness that, by chance, coincides with the moment of being offered it.

Once one has tried it, there is a new reason to take it again – how nice it is. More than this, it kills the other pleasures of life. By comparison, they lose their appeal. Heroin is a superbly effective trap: it drives the user ever deeper and the deeper he goes, the harder it is for him to extricate himself.

That 'normal' people can become addicted to heroin, which is why it is so dangerous, is one of the key points I want to get across. However, to read it is one thing; to believe it is another. You can even believe it in principle and yet not believe it could happen to your children. Most addicts never believed that it could happen to them; so many have said at one point: 'I'll never touch heroin', and, at another, 'I'll never get a habit. I only take it occasionally. I can handle it.'

In order to get this point across I have tried to generalise as much as possible. For this reason the book is not the story of any one person but contains quotes from some of the hundreds of people I know who have had experience of heroin in one form or another. Because heroin addiction is still, for the most part, regarded as a taboo subject, the quotes are unattributed. The special words that make up the language of heroin are explained in the Glossary.

To believe that heroin addiction can only happen to someone else's children is to ignore the size of the problem. In 1983, about 5,000 heroin addicts were notified to the Home Office. This is officially believed to be only one-fifth of the true figure and the number of heroin users is estimated to be between 10 and 20 times as great. This represents between 0.1–0.2 per cent of the population but, since at least 50 per cent of heroin users are between 15 and 25 years old, it represents 1 in every 200 of that age group. The figures are even higher in urban areas, where most heroin using is concentrated. In addition, the 1984 figures will show a 30–40 per cent increase.

That there can be so much ignorance in the face of such figures should not be possible, but people are ignorant about heroin because they want to be. Refusing to acknowledge the problem does not, unfortunately, make the problem go away; it allows it to become worse. An example of this ignorance is an article that I saw recently in the press, suggesting that heroin should be legalised. This is not as stupid as it sounds. The argument advanced was that it is not the drug itself that causes the damage but the addiction to it, its price forced artificially high by its illegal status, and the consequent need for money. The argument is based on the idea that it is not the business of the state to tell you what is good for you and what is not: if you never want to spend a moment sober, you have the right to make that decision.

It is certainly true that much of the social damage of heroin is the result of the addicts' need for money. If it only cost around £1 a gram, most of the crime associated with it would disappear. There the argument breaks down, through ignorance of the nature of the drug. Heroin is a mood-altering drug and, because a consistently experienced mood becomes part of the personality, it is also a personality-altering drug. By its chemical action it shuts out the rest of the world, making the user egocentric, selfish and irresponsive to the needs and wants of others. The Oxford English Dictionary suggests that its very name is derived from the Ancient Greek concept of the Tragic Hero as someone with an inflated notion of his own importance. How could a society even consider legalising a drug with such isolationist and anti-social effects? In addition, how does one protect the young, even with an age limit? The argument that we already have this difficulty with alcohol and that alcohol, too, can make people egocentric is merely a reason to outlaw it, not a reason to legalise heroin.

It should not be necessary to state that heroin is dangerous but, apparently, it is. I recently heard the reaction of a parent to a son's heroin taking: 'He was only having fun.' It is the word 'only' that turns the statement from an irrelevance into an absurdity. It is like saying that a young child playing with a loaded gun is only having fun. The child may be having fun but that is beside the point: he is also, like the heroin user, risking damage to himself and others and he is seemingly unaware of it.

Heroin is dangerous no matter how it is taken. It can be sniffed into the nose so that it enters the bloodstream through the nasal membrane; it can be smoked – known as 'chasing the dragon' – by melting it and inhaling the smoke; or it can be dissolved and injected, usually intravenously if a vein can be found, although it can be done intramuscularly or subcutaneously. Intravenous injection is the most physically damaging and dangerous method of administration. However, it is not the way heroin is taken that is addictive, it is the drug itself.

To take heroin once is to take a risk, the risk of liking it enough to take it again, the risk of becoming an addict. To take heroin is to risk one's health, one's liberty, even one's life. To take heroin is to take time out of life, time, which is the one irreplaceable commodity. The longer one takes out, the harder it is to pick up the pieces, to find a job, to find one's way back into the mainstream. Heroin forced me to abandon the good job I had. When I had stopped taking it, I had to go abroad to find another job. In order to obtain the work and resident's permits required I had to lie about my past, ignoring the warning at the bottom of the form describing what would happen if I made a false statement.

The damage of heroin is by no means confined to the users

themselves. It spreads out to involve the innocent. Those who have never taken heroin and probably never will suffer because someone else is taking it. Their very innocence lays them open to it. The most spectacular damage is financial. For example, the son of the butler in one of England's great country houses robbed the owner of tens of thousands of pounds by forging and cashing his cheques. And again:

'We had a chest in the cellar full of silver and silver-plate cups my grandfather had won, that sort of thing. The silver was pretty valuable and should really have been in the bank. We only occasionally got anything out of it, so we didn't notice for months that our son had broken into it. Somehow it just seems typical that he should have known the difference between the silver and the plate. He left us the plate. No insurance company was going to pay up because he was living at home. The only way we could get the silver back was to prosecute the shop that he had sold it all to for receiving stolen goods and that meant proving that they had known it was stolen. But we couldn't do that unless our son was first prosecuted for theft. We explained this to him and he was very good: he agreed to turn himself in, so I went with him to the police station. What was so sickening was that, after all that, the shopowners got off, though they were guilty. They must have been, the ridiculously low price they gave my son. They simply claimed they didn't know much about silver. What can you do?'

However great the financial damage, it is rarely as distressing as the emotional upset an addict can cause to those who love him.

'I went to see my son because he'd stopped coming to see me. I hadn't seen him in two months and in those two months he seemed to have changed completely. He just wasn't the same boy at all. We talked as if we were strangers. He didn't ask me how I was or how his Dad's back was, like he used to. He didn't even seem pleased to see me. I knew something was wrong but I thought it was his new girlfriend, who I didn't like the look of.'

'I kept missing money from my purse. It had to be one of the children. I didn't want to think it but I couldn't see who else it could be. Suddenly I couldn't trust them any more. It was awful. Where I grew up in the country we never even used to lock the house. Now to find that I had to be on my guard in my own house ... Is nowhere safe these days?'

'I went round to see my youngest daughter. When she opened the door, I thought she must be ill. She looked so pale and she seemed to have lost weight even though she was always skinny. But she said she felt fine. Oh God, why did I believe her? The night she came home to spend Christmas with us we found her in the bathroom. She hadn't even had time to pull the needle out of her arm.'

One of the strongest and most corrosive emotions often felt by parents is guilt. I remember telling my parents not to blame themselves, because I did not blame them. There is an unfortunate current trend to abnegate responsibility. How easy it is, armed with some dubious psychoanalysis, to claim that all one's faults are the result of being beaten or neglected as a child. Yet, if, by the age of 18, you cannot take responsibility for your own actions, how can you be considered responsible enough to choose a government, which, in this nuclear age, may be tantamount to deciding the fate of the human race?

My parents did not beat or neglect me. They were scrupulously fair and supportive. Because they grew up before experimentation with drugs became common in the 1960s, they were not in a position to know about them or warn me, except in the most general way. It was, I suppose, a traditional upbringing, the way they themselves were brought up. To use the same methods that worked in the past, however, only makes sense if the situation in the future is expected to be the same as it was in the past. My parents assumed it would be, because the enormous increase in the rate of change of scientific discovery and social structure and attitudes occurred in their lifetime.

Such an assumption is no longer valid. Life in twenty years' time will be different from life today. How it will differ it is difficult to predict. How many parents base their decision to have children on their idea of the sort of world their children will have to inhabit? It is as tempting for parents as it is for children to abnegate their responsibility. It may be difficult to predict the world their children will have to inhabit, but it must be a parent's duty to fit their children as well as possible for that world. That means keeping abreast of the changes, not ignoring them, even when, like heroin addiction, they are unpleasant.

I would like to think that this book could do more than show parents how to cope with the problem of heroin addiction once they have it. I would like to think that, by helping them to understand the reasons behind heroin taking, it could also show them ways in which they could prevent their children ever trying the drug. I would also like to think that the book could be useful to anyone – a friend, a relative, a doctor, a social worker – who has any contact with the problem of heroin taking. How can you help if you know little or nothing about the problem?

CHAPTER TWO

Availability

Heroin is easily obtainable in Britain, indeed anywhere in Western Europe, if you know what to look for. In almost any reasonable-sized town there is an area, or perhaps a pub, that local gossip claims is 'druggy'. One heroin user finds it comparatively easy to identify another. I used to know of two pubs in the King's Road in London where I could be fairly certain of finding either someone with heroin to sell or someone who knew where I could buy it. I would buy a drink and stand at the bar until I had spotted a likely-looking person. Then I would go over and sit beside him and casually ask him if he knew where I could buy some heroin. Sometimes I could not see anyone I thought was possible. I didn't once misjudge anyone so badly that they were outraged or didn't know what I was talking about.

'I was in a town I'd never been to before. It might have been Southampton but it happened to be Venice in Italy. Which only made it harder, because the only word of Italian I knew was "heroin." Luckily it was winter so there weren't many tourists about and Italians spend most of their time wandering about the streets so there were plenty of people to ask. No one told me to piss off – actually that's not quite true. One guy did and he was the only one I knew for certain was a junkie. I suppose it took about a couple of hours altogether to find the right bit of town and then to find a guy with smack. Of course it worked out pretty expensive, because it was sold in these ridiculous £5 bags – I had to buy a dozen to get about a third of a gram. Still, it was pretty good smack.'

The Customs & Excise estimate that they seize about 10 per cent of the total heroin traffic, but it may well be less. Last year they seized over 300 kilos. Even using their figure, this indicates a total volume of over 3 metric tonnes or, more significantly, since heroin is typically sold by the half, quarter or tenth of a gram, over 3 million grams.

This ready availability not only increases the likelihood that anyone will come into contact with it; it also makes it far harder to stop taking it or, once stopped, to stay off it. To know it is always there is to be continually tempted. This applies particularly to someone feeling the symptoms of heroin deprivation: he is in pain and he knows where the pain-killer is. Is it surprising that he does not resist the temptation?

> 'I wish I never knew smack existed. In fact, I wish it didn't exist. Once you know it's there, you can't just forget you know it. You can't even ignore it. I know I go on taking it but I still wish it didn't exist. Does that make sense?'

The words alone of the above quote do not, unfortunately, convey the despair in the voice of the girl who gave it to me. She died of a heroin overdose some time afterwards. Since she clearly saw the hopelessness of her predicament, I presume that she took the overdose deliberately. Her words are, to me, a plea for more effective measures to stop the flow of heroin.

Production

Heroin is a derivative of morphine, the principal alkaloid of opium. Opium itself is a gummy substance found in the seed pods of the opium poppy. When the petals have fallen, incisions are made in the pods, allowing the opium to ooze out. Collecting the opium is labour-intensive and the price in the countries where it is grown is low, so labour must be cheap. Opium poppies are hardy, produce one crop a year, and can be grown anywhere with a temperate or sub-tropical climate and a not excessive rainfall. Consequently they are often grown on poor soil in mountainous regions, where few other cash crops could survive.

The largest concentration of opium poppies is in an area known as the 'Golden Triangle', a mountainous region where Laos, Burma and Thailand meet. Other notable growing areas are in Mexico and Pakistan. Production in Iran, Turkey and Afghanistan has fallen following recent political events.

The largest upsurge in heroin availability in Britain coincided with the Iranian Revolution. In the face of growing civil unrest, many of the Iranian middle class decided to leave the country. The shortage of time often made it impossible for them to realise their assets held inside Iran. Many could get out with only what they could carry. To compensate for what they were forced to leave behind, some decided to invest in heroin, a transaction that offered enormous profits. In addition, heroin has a higher value to weight or volume ratio than a £10 note. Because of the liberal political climate in Britain, many Iranians settled here. For a while there was a glut of prime-quality heroin available, until the market expanded to absorb it. However, as a result of this glut, it was impossible to sell heroin that had been too heavily adulterated. Consequently a tradition of high purity grew up in Britain so that, on average, it is much purer than in the US. It also introduced smoking as a method of administration, which made heroin taking more widely acceptable.

Following the Iranian Revolution, heroin possession was made a capital offence. Britain's major source of supply moved north to Afghanistan and then, after the Russian invasion, north again to Pakistan. Afghanistan is still producing heroin, but it is sold almost exclusively to the occupying Russian army.

Attempts by the Western nations, and, in particular the US because of its economic power, to halt the growing of opium poppies worldwide have been largely unsuccessful. First efforts were almost wholly abortive. Financial incentives were offered through the governments of the countries concerned to substitute other crops for the poppies. The financial influence, however, proved less strong than the influence of the opium buyers. These opium buyers whose profits allowed them to employ armed gangs, were more persuasive than the dollar to the opium-growing communities, often isolated in inaccessible mountain regions. Then too, US influence was badly damaged by the Vietnam War, especially in the East. Not only did they lose it but, during its course, a significant number of American troops were buying heroin. According to two US Congress members, 10–15 per cent of GIs were using heroin in Vietnam in 1971. Worse than this, a US government agency was involved in covert operations that encouraged the opium trade: the CIA flew out shipments of opium for certain hill tribes in order to persuade them to fight the North Vietnamese. After the war, the US Drug Enforcement Agency engaged in the self-defeating policy of offering to buy opium at current prices and then destroying it. Inevitably the new buyer in the market simply encouraged increased production.

Marginally more successful has been the recent policy of putting pressure on the governments of the opium-growing countries to take their own preventative measures. The usual form of pressure has been economic and military aid. By tying this to effective action against opium, the US has forced these governments to do something. However, it is not easy for them. The growing areas are frequently inaccessible and guarded by armed men so that expensive airborne military operations are required. In addition, for the growing communities, the crop represents their only form of subsistence. Finally, corruption is so endemic, so culturally integrated, particularly in the East, that the opium buyers can often buy protection of the crop. Action against the buyers themselves rather than the crop is complicated by their mobility. Even though they often do the refining themselves, it does not hamper this mobility: two chemists and a small amount of equipment is all that is necessary to isolate the morphine, which makes up approximately 10 per cent of opium, and refine it into heroin.

However, these governments need Western aid. Consequently they have a tendency to arrange from time to time a showpiece crop burning, well rehearsed and well attended by the press. They get their aid, Western drug enforcement agencies feel that they are achieving something and Western governments can point out to their electorates that they are taking positive action against the drug menace. Meanwhile the heroin trade continues.

Importation

The large-scale importers of heroin make fortunes. Importation is the most profitable stage of the trade. A kilo of heroin costs £1000 or less in Pakistan. In Britain it can be sold for between £60,000 and £100,000, without being adulterated, if it is sold in lots of 1 gram or less, or for about £35,000 if it is sold by the ounce. With this scale of profits the big importers can afford to insulate themselves from any connection with the trade so that they run no risk of arrest: their only risk is financial. They can afford to pay people – 'runners' – to carry the drugs through customs for them and others to collect them and sell them. They need never see the drugs themselves.

Equally they have the resources to set up innocent people to do the carrying. This requires more organisation than using 'runners', but it is cheaper. It has the added advantage that innocent people, when they walk through customs, generally look innocent. I know of one girl who apparently did not look innocent enough. She went on holiday to Thailand, where she met and had an affair with a Chinese man. She was stopped at the airport by the Thai police before boarding the plane for her return journey. They found over 5 kilos of heroin in her suitcase. Even though she was almost certainly innocent, the Chinese man had, unsurprisingly, disappeared, so she had no defence. The court was lenient: the death sentence was commuted to life imprisonment.

With enough money it is possible to avoid customs altogether, by using, for example, boats to land the drugs on remote stretches of coastline. It is also possible to set up import-export companies to bring the drugs in, hidden in manufactured goods.

'I took my dealer round to see the man he scored off. I was amazed that he let me come in, because normally people like that are so paranoid. Anyway he disappeared into the kitchen and came back with a chair leg. There weren't lion's feet at the bottom or anything but I swear it was a chair leg. He got a screwdriver and knocked out these little plugs and out came smack. Of course, it had a few bits of wood in it. Typically my dealer said: "Oh man, I didn't come here to score sawdust." I kept wanting to go into the kitchen to see how many legs this chair had left.'

Large-scale drug importation has become very politicised. In the Eastern Mediterranean and the Middle East it has become a common practice to use drugs, especially heroin, to finance the purchase of arms. For example, certain groups in Eastern Turkey financed their insurgency operations with heroin so successfully that law and order had almost totally broken down in Turkey before the military coup in 1980. Heavily involved in this trade and offering both safe meeting places and transport facilities is Bulgaria. Both drugs and arms are destabilising to the West, and through certain drug and arms dealers, Bulgaria was inextricably linked to the plot to kill the Pope.

The big importers do not, in Britain, have the stranglehold on the heroin trade that they have in, for example, the US, partly because there is far less organised crime in Britain. A significant proportion of Britain's heroin is imported by 'solo operators'. These individuals typically do the buying, the importing and, sometimes, the selling themselves. Consequently they run far higher risks. Even the buying is not risk free: sellers have been known to tip off the police, for example because they have themselves been arrested and wish to trade names for leniency.

'I only did three runs and the most I brought back at a time was 5 ounces. I'd take an ounce at a time, wrap it in three Durex and swallow it. Durex are the best thing, because they keep the dope tight-packed and they're strong enough to withstand the stomach acids for long enough. The one thing you don't want is 5 ounces of dope bursting in your stomach. My one fear was that the plane would be delayed once I'd got on it.'

It is almost impossible for the Customs to spot smugglers, who have long learnt that they are much more likely to be searched if they have long messy hair and dirty jeans and come off a plane from Bombay than if they change planes and appear to be sales executives arriving from Brussels. In addition, smugglers are often extremely inventive in their choice of hiding place for the drugs. It is a historical fact that, if enough resources are applied to a problem, a solution will be found. This applies as much to smuggling as it does to putting a man on the moon.

The resources for heroin smuggling are indubitably there: the profits are enormous, although less than press reports would suggest. These reports price Customs' seizures at 'street' value, which is what the users will eventually pay. No one, however, who has just brought 10 kilos into the country is going to spend every day of the next three years selling it in quarter-gram lots. It is surprising, in the face of the inventiveness that the profits can buy, that the Customs stop as much as they do. Most of the large seizures are the result of prior information or tip-offs. At last the Customs have put one of their men in Pakistan to aid this flow of information. This will help to stop the smugglers, but it will do little to combat the big importers. As the 'solo operators' are taken out of the trade so the gaps will increasingly be filled by organised crime. Already the IRA are involved in heroin trading to finance their operations. The Customs are fighting a losing war.

Dealing

A heroin dealer is anyone who regularly sells heroin. Depending on the size of an imported batch, it may pass through the hands of middlemen before it reaches the 'street' dealers, who sell it directly to the users. Because of the irregularity of supply there is no neat, pyramidical structure of dealers. The differentiation between middlemen and 'street' dealers frequently breaks down, particularly when the dealer uses heroin himself, as is frequently the case.

'I had this dealer I used to score off, sometimes just a tenner's, even a fiver's worth. Then I stopped for a while and when I next went to see him to score I asked for a quarter [of a gram]. He told me he wasn't doing less than 3 grams at a time. He let me have the quarter just that once but I couldn't score off him regularly. Then a couple of months later, he rang me up and asked if I could score for him, because he was sick and couldn't get any.'

I know of one dealer who recently moved up from 'street' dealing to dealing in bulk because it involves fewer, more reliable customers and so is less risky. He had come to the attention of the police following his presence at the death of a woman from heroin and cocaine he had provided.

'Street' dealing does not necessarily take place on the street. Britain is much less of a street culture than, say, the Mediterranean countries; so much of the dealing is done from the dealer's home. This is not to say that street dealing does not exist: a walk up Shaftesbury Avenue from Piccadilly Circus in London should convince you of that. However, users do not like buying on the street; it gives them too little chance of examining what they are buying and, because the seller is often quick to disappear, too little chance of redress. I've watched a friend buying a small packet of what was almost exclusively baking powder for £20.

Dealers are consistently vilified in the press. A better target would be the big importers, who are involved in the trade only for the money they can make out of it and are fully aware of the misery they are causing. This vilification of dealers frequently uses the emotive word 'pusher'. Properly, a 'pusher' is someone who encourages others to take heroin by giving it to them and, then, when they are addicted, refuses to let them have any more unless they pay for it. He does this exclusively to increase his clientele and so make more money. Many dealers, on the contrary, turn away new clients, because more clients mean more risk. Equally, as a general rule people are not introduced to heroin by a dealer; they are introduced by their best friends. 'Pushers' probably exist, but I have never come across one or met anyone who has. To equate 'pushing' with dealing is another example of the ignorance that besets the whole subject of heroin. The subject is already emotive enough without the use of words like 'pusher'.

I do not wish to seem to be defending dealers. However, to say that all dealers are evil is as false as most such all-embracing generalisations. It is the equivalent of saying that all German soldiers in the last world war were evil. Correctly, evil refers to motivation not action: unless he wanted to do so, a surgeon who kills a patient while operating on him is not evil.

The motivation for a dealer is often not primarily money: dealing is simply a way to ensure that he has enough heroin for himself. He is not doing it to become rich.

'You want to know why I deal? You know how old I am? I'll be 40 this year. I went to public school, you know. I even went to university. I even had a job for a while, but in the 'sixties I got into smack. It got to the point where I was really living hand to mouth or, maybe I should say, needle to arm. I suppose at that point I might have stopped but by then I was nearly 30. It seemed too late to go back to being straight. There's only so much of your life you can throw away. So I started dealing seriously. At least this way I've got enough smack and just about enough money to live all right. Most of the time, anyway. Of course, I've been busted twice so I suppose, if they get me again I'll go down for quite a long time. Please don't ask me what I'd do if I had my life over again – that's too stupid a question even to bother with.'

A dealer I knew refused at one point to sell me any more. He saw that I had begun to come to see him every day. He thought I was just becoming addicted. He told me: 'Look, you've got a chance. You could do something with your life. These other poor fuckers they're all no-hopers: they ain't go no chance. You gotta stop now before you can't.' I pleaded with him and pointed out that by then I'd been addicted for more than a year, which was true; I'd just been buying elsewhere. He wouldn't listen to me. He pressed some methadone pills into my hand to help me stop and threw me out. I was furious: I didn't want a lecture; I wanted some heroin.

Some dealers do not make money; they may even lose it. Either they themselves take too much of what they are supposed to be selling; or they give too much credit, perhaps because they feel they must do something for an addict suffering the symptoms of deprivation. Giving credit to addicts is poor business, because it is rarely repaid. Addicts tend to extend the credit as much as possible and then find a new dealer with whom they can make a fresh start. Just before I stopped taking heroin I ran up a credit of over £200 with a dealer. After I had stopped I had no difficulty in justifying to myself never paying him back. Dealers can be the victims of addicts as much as anyone else.

Another reason some dealers do not make money is inefficiency. It is excruciating for an addict to go to see his dealer and find that the dealer is out when he said he would be in, or fell asleep when he should have been buying some more and so does not have any, or cannot be bothered to answer the door because he has just taken some and wants to relax. After I stopped taking heroin, I frequently had the same nightmare, in which I went to see a dealer. When I arrived, he told me that he had just sold the last of his heroin. In the nightmare the person he had sold it to was on the

point of leaving as I arrived. It is a paradox that, although heroin is
so readily available, it is often very difficult to buy at the moment
one wants it.

'I went round to my dealer's, because he'd promised the night
before that he'd have some. Did he? So he asked me to drive him
to get some more. Of course, it was miles away. By the time we
got there it was already 11 p.m. and I'd promised to be home by
midnight. So I said to him: "Look, if you're going to be more
than half an hour, for Christ's sake come out and tell me." I sat
in the car 'till 3.00 a.m. and then he hadn't got any. I could've
killed him. How the fuck can someone spend four hours *not*
scoring?'

There is money to be made from dealing. Heroin can currently
be bought for £40 or less per gram for 3–5 grams and resold at
around £80 a gram. Profits can be increased by adulterating it –
known as 'cutting' it – or by weighing out short measures: it is easy
to tamper with a pair of scales so that they do not weigh true. Some
dealers do not use scales, preferring to measure amounts by eye or
sell packets of a fixed value, such as £10: scales are *prima facie*
evidence of possession with intent to supply, which carries a higher
sentence than simple possession. However, experienced dealers can
measure by eye as accurately as all but the best scales.

Typically, it is the dealer who is only interested in making
money who is the most efficient and therefore preferred by addicts.

'I knew this guy who used to come to London and take a flat for
six months. He used to deal only between 6 and 8 each evening
but he was always there and he always had stuff. He was pretty
expensive – he charged a hundred quid a g. – but it was worth it,
because you knew you weren't gonna be pissed around. He
hardly ever took it himself and after six months he'd made
enough to do nothing for the next six months. Then he'd be back
in another place. He reckoned it cut down his risk of being busted.'

Although a dealer is primarily motivated either by the need to support his own addiction or by money, there are often other, subsidiary reasons. A dealer has standing in the heroin community; he is important to his addict customers: they literally need him. Above all, he has power.

'I can't bear dealers who get off on this power kick. They start playing God and you have to bow and scrape or they won't let you score. I've seen it happen to perfectly decent guys. They start dealing and suddenly they turn into real bastards, ordering everyone around and being a pain in the neck. I suppose it's being surrounded by whining junkies begging for credit all the time that does it.'

Just as there are some dealers who are genuinely kind and scrupulously careful about not introducing anyone to heroin or selling to anyone they consider too young, so there are those who ruthlessly exploit the power that heroin gives them.

Most dealing is done from home, because it is easier. However, it involves more risk. Sometimes, therefore, dealers work out systems of meeting their clients. One dealer I knew used to catch the London underground from Putney Bridge station, which was near where she lived, at about 6 each evening. At each stop she got off, sold to anyone waiting there, and took the next train on. At Gloucester Road she turned round and repeated the procedure on the way back.

'When I was dealing, I used to score 10 grams at a time. I'd ring my man to arrange to meet him on a certain corner at a certain time. About a quarter of an hour before I was due to arrive – I know, because I once got there early and watched – he'd walk round the block and throw a cigarette packet under a parked car. Then, when I arrived, we'd walk round the block together and I'd give him the money. At that point neither of us had any gear on us so it didn't matter if we got stopped and searched and, anyway, we could see if we were being watched. Then he'd say it's in a cigarette packet under the blue Escort or whatever.'

Another dealer I knew rented an 'office' that he used exclusively for dealing.

A dealer's risk increases with the number of people he sells to: any one of them may be arrested for possession of heroin and give his name to the police. Most arrests of dealers happen that way. Typically, an addict will be stopped in connection with some other offence, for example driving through a red light. A search follows and a packet of heroin is found. The police then put pressure on the addict for the name of his supplier. Where possible, the police like to arrest addicts on Friday evenings so that they will not appear in court until Monday: this leaves the whole weekend for the addict to feel the symptoms of deprivation.

'When they busted me, the first question was: "Where did you buy it?" It was a Saturday morning and by Sunday I was feeling sick. They kept on at me. They even offered me some smack if I told them, but, in the first place, I didn't believe them and, anyway, I've been sick before and the dealer I'd scored off is a friend of mine. There was no way I was going to tell . them.'

In order to reduce the number of clients and the frequency of their visits to his house (because this may make neighbours curious), a dealer may operate a stepped pricing policy. So he may charge, for example, £25 for a quarter of a gram, £40 for a half, and £70 for a whole gram. This encourages the users either to club together or to buy enough for two or three days at a time.

The risks for dealers are not as great as they should be. A sturdy door and good locks often give a dealer the time to dispose of most of his heroin while the police are trying to break in. He will almost certainly leave traces and so will be prosecuted for possession, which rarely results in more than a fine. In the absence of other evidence, such as scales, he will probably beat a charge of possession with intent to supply.

What can be done

Judging from the Customs' seizure figures, around 50 per cent more heroin entered Britain in 1984 than in 1983. Over the same period, the number of heroin addicts notified to the Home Office rose by 30–40 per cent. Britain's heroin problem is not only increasing; it is increasing rapidly. There is a pressing need for more resources to fight it.

It is almost impossible to move effectively against either the opium growers or the importers. Opium growing takes place in foreign countries, so that effective action depends on the cooperation of the governments of those countries, a cooperation that is, at best, suspect. Importers will always be successful in a large proportion of their attempts at smuggling: it is impracticable to search everyone who passes through Customs, or even a significant proportion, particularly at the busier ports of entry, which are therefore favoured by smugglers. However, something could be done to improve the situation if the government stopped thinking of the Customs as tax collectors and recognised them as a law enforcement agency. They need an increase, or at least a reorganisation, of manpower so that more Customs officers are available to fight the flood of heroin. One man in Pakistan is not enough nor are the forty who make up the five heroin investigative units that have to cover the whole of Britain.

The links in the chain that are most susceptible to pressure, then, are the dealers. If dealing was much more difficult and hazardous, heroin would become less available. This would lower the number of people who come into contact with it and so try it for the first time. Also, because the difficulty of obtaining it would weigh against the pleasure of taking it, fewer users would continue to take it and more addicts would consider it easier and more worthwhile to stop. Such action would also affect the profitability of importation, since, with supply outlets limited, a given amount would take longer to sell. As profitability declined, importers would tend to move away from the trade, thereby lowering availability still more. Just as there is a vicious upward spiral whereby the more that is available, the more the market expands to absorb it, so the reverse is true: the less that is available, the greater the contraction of the market.

Police drug squads are under-manned for the task that confronts them. In the current economic climate it is unlikely that their budget will be significantly increased. Therefore, the resources that are available must be concentrated on heroin, even if this means to a large extent neglecting the other drugs. Heroin *is* the most socially damaging drug and its use presents a far more serious and pressing problem that that of any other drug, with the possible exception of barbiturates and solvents, which are mostly outside the scope of the drug squads. A complete suppression of heroin is desirable, even at the expense, of some proliferation of other drugs. In addition, the drug squads should not be hampered by other considerations. In some areas, the drug squads are not allowed to raid premises, even though they know that drugs are sold there, for fear of provoking riots. This seems to me to be tantamount to a licence to deal.

One of the difficulties the police face is their inability to infiltrate effectively the heroin world: even in plain clothes they do not look like heroin users. Consequently they often have to rely on the chance arrest of an addict and their ability to exploit his addiction to make him reveal the source of his heroin. Young or inexperienced addicts often talk, whereas long-time addicts and dealers rarely do; they are experienced enough to know that they can endure heroin deprivation if they have to. Consequently police action tends only to be effective against the bottom of the distribution network and then only temporarily. One dealer is arrested and another soon appears to fill his place. This happens because the current police manpower shortage allows only periodic crack-downs on particular areas. In the intervening lulls, the distribution networks re-form. The only way to suppress heroin dealing is to apply continuous pressure.

The government is currently considering stiffer penalties for heroin dealing – a maximum sentence of life imprisonment for possession with intent to supply, together with powers to enable the courts to confiscate drug profits. I feel this will deter dealers far less than would continuous police pressure and a consequently greater risk of arrest. The police might, however, be able to use these harder penalties as a lever to make some progress towards the top of the distribution network by offering to exercise a discretion not to prosecute only for the lesser offence of simple possession in exchange for the name of the dealer's supplier.

But what of the dealer who deals only to addicts, who has never introduced anyone to heroin, who makes no money from it and who does it only to support his own addiction? Such dealers exist. Do they deserve life imprisonment? Do they deserve it, even if they refuse to name their supplier, which they may be too scared of reprisals to do? It might be felt that the protection of society requires that a few be treated unfairly. It is not, however, at all certain that stiffer penalties will have any material effect on heroin availability.

It may be that the law enforcement approach is not the way to tackle the problem. Certainly it will never be able to suppress heroin completely. It may be that the way to attack the supply is through demand: if a way can be found to stop people wanting the drug, the supply will dwindle of its own accord.

CHAPTER THREE

Willingness

The question, 'Why does someone try heroin?', lies at the heart of the heroin problem. The mountaineers' answer, 'Because it is there', is inadequate as an explanation. Its availability provides the opportunity; it does not provide the necessary willingness to try it.

Some who try heroin undoubtedly have a strong desire to do so; they want to try it as soon as they encounter it. A few have such unpleasant lives that they will try anything that promises relief or escape. A few possess that reckless curiosity that requires sampling everything. A few take everything on offer in a search for something they cannot identify.

> 'Looking back, I think I was aware that there was something missing in my life. I didn't know what I was looking for. In fact I don't think I really knew I was looking for anything. But there was definitely something wrong with my life. It wasn't – I suppose satisfying is the word. And I was doing all these bizarre things. If someone asked me if I wanted to try hang-gliding or smack or whatever, I'd say yes at once, without thinking whether it might be dumb or dangerous. Of course, in the end I realised smack wasn't the answer I was looking for; but it made me forget I had a question.'

A few, too, always go looking for trouble: they will do something simply because it is illegal.

Most of those who try heroin, however, do not have a positive drive to do so; rather they acquiesce. The willingness to try heroin can amount to as little as an inability to say no. The determinants of this acquiescence differ, at least in detail, in each case. Indeed, even for those with a strong motivation to try heroin, what lies behind that motivation is as different as the personality and circumstances of each individual. So, for example, the quote above is only a superficial explanation for trying heroin. It raises the questions: what was missing from his life? Why did he look for it outside of himself and particularly in a chemical? Why was he not aware at the time that he was looking for something? It is questions such as these that must be answered in order to understand heroin and to be able to do something about it.

In order to generalise and to see some of the problem areas that can lead to heroin, the question, 'Why does someone try heroin?', has to be answered negatively. Simply put, people try heroin because they do not have sufficient reason not to do so. They do not have strong psychological barriers to it, just as its ready availability does not constitute a sufficient physical barrier.

These psychological barriers, which are, or should be, erected by upbringing and education, are anything that tends to prevent someone trying heroin. For example, a proper understanding of the drug and what it does can be a deterrent. They can also be of the type that leads people away from heroin. So those with ambition or religious faith are less likely to come into contact with it or to be interested in trying something of such an escapist nature.

However strong these barriers, they can be shattered by set-backs, by pressure, by the death of someone close. They can also be eroded by time: the once-learned warnings about heroin can lose their force over the years. One can also break down the barriers oneself little by little by breaking one after another of one's own rules until the whole structure of resistance crumbles. Very few are lucky enough never to experience moments of weakness, self-doubt and vulnerability. It is often tempting in these moments to escape into a haze of alcohol, pills or powders. The ability to refuse the easy way out depends on another sort of psychological barrier – the internal resources of self-confidence and strength of character.

Whether a moment of weakness coincides with the moment of

being offered heroin is so often purely a matter of chance. The role of chance in the creation of an addict is frequently ignored when, in fact, it can be crucial. It is one of the chief arguments against the thesis that no 'normal' person would take heroin. Clearly, however, the weaker an individual's barriers and the longer his periods of vulnerability, the less important is the role of chance.

Barriers

To know about heroin and its dangers should be enough to deter anyone from trying it. Very few are capable of taking it with the care necessary to avoid addiction. Those few are typically capable of controlling their drug use only because of circumstances in which the higher priorities of other aspects of their life limit the occasions of drug use. If those circumstances change, addiction can follow. In other words, one has a statistically poor chance of avoiding the progression from trying heroin and liking it to becoming addicted.

Even this simple, basic fact about the addictive nature of heroin is almost universally ignored or misunderstood. Most people, before they try heroin, are aware that it is addictive but do not seem able to understand what that means. They think that addiction will not happen to them. This typifies the state of knowledge of the entire subject. Even when the facts are known, they are either not understood or not believed.

Formal drug education is almost non-existent in Britain. What knowledge there is frequently comes from people who are involved with drugs themselves and it is therefore often laced with the misinformed mythology of the drug culture and biased by personal experience. Ignorance is consequently widespread.

'When I first tried smack, I was expecting, you know, stars and stripes like with LSD. I don't know where I got that idea from; I suppose someone must have told me or, maybe, I'd somehow got the idea that that's what all "hard" drugs did.'

Exhortations of the 'Don't touch it' variety without a reasoned, informed explanation can be counter-productive. Children, in particular, have a tendency to mirror the thinking of Adam in the Garden of Eden: if I'm not supposed to touch it, it must be good.

In the absence of education, knowledge about heroin is often absorbed from the newspapers, which is the equivalent of learning about Britain by listening to Russian radio broadcasts. When they are not misinformed, the newspapers' emphasis on interest and sensationalism tends to distort the facts. This sensationalism, even when concentrated on the most sordid aspects of addiction, often perversely has the effect of glamourising heroin. I have recently come across two people who boasted to me that they had been heroin addicts. A little probing showed this to be quite untrue, so I can only assume they thought it was 'smart' to have been an addict.

The widespread use of drugs in the entertainment world has become a tradition and, more importantly, is well publicised: every year a number of pop and film stars are involved publicly with drugs. They are arrested; they take overdoses; or they go for cures. There is no lack of films or pop songs about drugs. So, for example, the song *Heroin* gives a fair picture of the drug. However, the lines that are critical of the drug are more difficult to understand, unless one already knows about it, than lines such as, 'Cos it makes me feel like I'm a man / When I put a spike into my vein'.* Indeed, to some extent just to write a song about heroin glamorises it. The association between the drug and the pop world is enough.

The illegality of heroin would be a sufficient deterrent, were there a universal respect for the law and belief in the need to uphold it. Yet how many people now see the police as there to catch them rather than to protect them? It is not considered wrong to avoid

---

*From the song *Heroin* composed by Lou Reed.
Lyrics reproduced by permission of RCA Music Ltd.

paying taxes by exploiting legal loopholes, even though those loopholes are the result of the draughtsman's error and the intention of the law is clear. Millions of pounds in revenue is lost each year because car and television licence fees are not paid. The state is no longer seen as a collection of people; it has grown into an identity of its own. There is a consequent feeling that it, and so the law, its instrument, is owed a much lower standard of morality than a nextdoor neighbour or friend. Children very rarely have a higher morality than their parents.

There has been an observable, general decline in morality over the course of this century and particularly since the last world war. Morality as a code of conduct by which to live is much stronger if it is adopted and believed by the individual than if it is imposed. The reason so few of the young have a strong sense of morality is that its traditional foundation, Christianity, has collapsed. Christian ethics no longer seem relevant to a materialist culture: giving to the poor seems to be at odds with amassing as many possessions as possible. The young, therefore, tend no longer to feel within themselves that something is 'wrong'; instead they are *told* it is 'wrong'. This lacks the force and the ability to restrain of a belief.

Ambition acts as a barrier by pushing people in a direction away from drugs. And, indeed, the majority of heroin addicts admit to lacking any strong ambition before they tried heroin. Indubitably the current economic situation has much to answer for: it is hard to be ambitious if one has no hope of fulfilling that ambition.

'Everyone goes on at me to stop taking smack, And do what? Where am I going to find a job? Everyone round here's on the dole. You think it's fun living in this shitty area? What future have I got? At least on smack I don't have to care about it. Of course I deal. How else am I going to support a habit?'

Yet the lack of jobs is not the whole answer. Driving ambition can overcome the job shortage. However there is in general little strong desire for anything amongst the young. Behind this apathy lies the failure of materialism to provide a sufficiently attractive, ultimate goal: to own two cars and a suburban house is not enough.

The experimentation with drugs that expanded so rapidly in the 1960s was a reflection of this feeling that pound notes were not a proper measure of the value of life. During that period the use of drugs to expand the consciousness was closely connected with a search for a spiritual quality in life, and, in particular, mystical experience. This led to the flowering in the West of religions, such as Buddhism, with a stronger mystical tradition than Christianity. What mysticism Christianity possessed has been increasingly submerged beneath attempts to explain the religion. There is today an undoubted spiritual vacuum in the West often experienced as an unidentifiable need. Heroin seems to fill that need.

Knowing how to find pleasure and enjoyment without drugs of any kind is one of the best barriers to heroin. Yet the education system does not encourage this; rather the opposite. With its insistence on the need to specialise early to get the exams to get a job, it does not allow the broad experimentation necessary to discover what one enjoys doing. A good job is not a well-paid job; it is an enjoyable one.

In a time of massive unemployment, clearly an enjoyable job is an ideal. Consequently, outside interests as a source of pleasure – whether they be political, sporting, crafts, in fact of any sort – are the more important. It is surprising how often those of the unemployed with a keen interest turn that interest into a way to make money. These interests require encouragement and development in childhood and so often do not receive it.

A barrier to heroin is anything that provides enjoyment, satisfaction or fulfilment, anything that risks being sacrificed to heroin. The less there is to be sacrificed, whether principles or time or money, the easier it is to succumb.

Weakness

The weakness of one's barriers increases one's susceptibility to heroin. However, even the strongest barriers break down from time to time. The most ambitious person can lose his drive, the most religious his faith, in the face of an emotional crisis. The death of someone close can temporarily make life seem pointless and without interest and increase one's vulnerability to escapism.

Very few people are lucky enough to avoid depression at some point in their lives. It is easier to bear if one knows that it will pass, but that knowledge is only acquired through experience. Whatever one is told, the first major set-back of life often seems unsurmountable.

'I had this friend. His father died when he was about 18, I think, and his family's affairs sort of dropped into his lap: there was this great house that was falling down and no money and three or four kids, I think, to be educated. He started using to forget about it all. I think he saw the rest of his life as slaving to keep a roof on the house, like his father's had been. Anyway, smack wasn't really the answer for him: he needed something more permanent by way of solution. Which he found with a shotgun.'

Depression does not necessarily have dramatic beginnings. I went through a two-month depression as a result of a trivial incident. I threw a piece of paper away as I was walking along a street. Then I stopped and went back to pick it up, because it had suddenly occurred to me that trees were providing this paper: forests were being cut down so that I could litter the streets. The more I thought about it, the more the whole way we live seemed wrong. I began to see only the dark side of everything: cars no longer signified transport but pollution of the air and crude oil suffocating coastlines instead; the leftovers from a restaurant tipped into a dustbin made me think of the starving; in a pet I could see only the domestication of the wild, man's interference with nature; electricity cables meant not warmth and light but nuclear waste spilling into the sea. I felt wholly powerless to prevent the unfolding spectacle of human disintegration and I wasn't at all sure I wanted to stay and watch.

Pressure can be just as debilitating as depression, whether it be the pressure of a strained love affair or the pressure of work. Pressure increases the need for relaxation, if not escape. Real relaxation of tension consists of more than simply putting one's feet up. Consequently the idea of a chemical that effortlessly provides such a relaxing of tension can be seductive. The widespread use of alcohol and tranquillisers attests to the perceived need for chemical release.

The pressure of opinion can be a key factor in a decision to try heroin. It requires a certain maturity to be able to refuse something one's friends are taking, without implying either a criticism of them or fear on one's own part. It requires self-confidence to refuse and not care what they think.

'The first time I tried heroin I was with a bunch of mates. They were all smoking it. When they offered me some I didn't want to refuse because I didn't want to make a big thing of it. It was just easier to accept. I guess I was a bit scared, but they kept saying it was all right. I guess that reassured me.'

Taking heroin is sometimes perceived as setting one apart from the ordinary. It can create the feeling of belonging to a secret society. It has its own customs and language, unknown to the uninitiated. So those without the barrier of a strong sense of their own worth or identity are more vulnerable.

For someone with a reasonable resistance to trying heroin, one period of weakness, unless it is extended, will not be enough. Typically, however, resistance to heroin begins as resistance to drugs in general. Consequently, resistance to heroin is weakened when the resistance to other drugs is weakened. The barriers to heroin can be almost removed before heroin is ever on offer.

It is an often-stated maxim that 'soft' drugs (principally cannabis) lead to 'hard' drugs such as amphetamines, barbiturates, cocaine and heroin. The reason given is that people are looking for even better 'kicks'. Apparently one only discovers this urge for 'kicks' after trying cannabis (This argument has been used to justify keeping cannabis illegal.) The specious evidence employed is the undoubted fact that most heroin users have tried cannabis first, whereas very few cannabis users tried heroin first.

This reasoning is wrong. Cannabis does not give one the desire for 'kicks'. More than this, most people are not looking for 'kicks'. Typically, they come across a drug, find that they like it, and continue to use it. Nor do they think, 'Oh, I'm bored of cannabis, I must go and look for a better high.' Boredom with cannabis may make someone more willing to try heroin, which is a different statement. It is saying that boredom, rather than cannabis, is a cause of heroin use.

The major fallacy of the argument is that the 'kick' or 'high' of one drug is better than another. For example, cannabis increases sensory and emotional awareness, while playing havoc with rational thought, whereas cocaine stimulates the rational processes. They thus suit different people. Again, cocaine is a stimulant whereas heroin is a depressant. To compare them is like comparing black and white. Indeed, even when they are most comparable – when they are injected so that the immediate effect, the 'rush', disguises their differences – it would be wrong to say that heroin is better. On the contrary, the 'rush' from cocaine is better, both in my personal experience and that of everyone I know who has tried both.

Were heroin truly better than cannabis and drug users only concerned with 'kicks', the vast majority of cannabis users would become heroin users, since heroin is available, if one looks for it. The figures do not bear this out. There are between 1 and 3 million cannabis users in Britain and between 50,000 and 100,000 heroin users. The reason that the progression is from cannabis to heroin and not vice-versa is partly due to the fact that cannabis is even more readily available than heroin so that it is generally encountered first. In addition, heroin ruins other drugs. Being a depressant, it produces an edginess or nervousness when it is not being taken. This uncomfortable sensation may be only a psychosomatic effect induced by mental comparison with the state of relaxation produced by the drug, but it is none the less exacerbated by cannabis and particularly by stimulants such as cocaine and amphetamines.

More than this, heroin tends to be the ultimate drug in the progression because it is addictive. It does not allow users the freedom to move on to other drugs.

Yet there is a connection between 'soft' and 'hard' drugs. Many people, before they encounter drugs at all, have a barrier both against drugs and against breaking the law. By trying cannabis, they inevitably weaken that barrier. By continuing to use it, they weaken the barrier still further. They put themselves continually outside the law so that law-breaking no longer seems so bad. They also come into contact with an illegal world in which dealers often sell more than one type of drug. This makes it much more likely that they will encounter other drugs.

'I've been smoking dope now for ten years. I remember one evening I was round my dealer's scoring and there was this other guy there. They'd been to school together or something. Anyway we sat around rapping and getting stoned and I noticed that this other guy only took a really quick toke before passing the joint on, like he was just being polite and didn't really want to get stoned. Then he produced this packet and asked us if we'd like a line of smack. Well I had an elder brother who died of a heroin overdose so you can imagine that it's not exactly my favourite stuff. I'd like to see smack dealers shot. But I wasn't exactly going to ring the law, was I? I mean: "Come round and bust this junkie and while you're here have a toke of one of these very fine Thai sticks my friend here's got two hundred of stashed behind the sink."'

The fact that 'soft' drugs can lead to 'hard' drugs by weakening both mental and physical barriers is thus an argument for legalising cannabis. Decriminalisation is not the answer, because it appears to sanction personal use while doing nothing about the vast criminal profits or the illegality that tends to lead to encounters with 'hard' drugs. It is beyond the scope of this book to discuss the desirability of legalising cannabis, for example as the Dutch have done, making it legally available at youth clubs. However, it would not be inconsistent to legalise cannabis and, simultaneously, introduce tougher measures against other drugs, paricularly heroin. This would then be seen as a realignment, rather than a relaxation, of attitudes. A tax on cannabis might even be used to finance an increase in Customs and drug squad manpower.

Chance

Chance is so often the link between availability and willingness. Certainly some people have no barriers and are always willing to try whatever is offered. Even so, it is possible never to come into contact with heroin. It is a mistake to dismiss the importance of chance. It is too easy in retrospect to discern a pattern that seems to lead inevitably to heroin addiction.

'I'd started taking gear and I was quite into it. I didn't have a habit but I was going that way. Then I got invited to this party. I went off to score before the party and it took hours and in the end I didn't get any. I was very pissed off, because I really thought the party would be a drag without it. But the party just happened to be on my way home, so I thought I might as well stop in for five minutes. Well I met this chick there and she was *fan-tastic*. So we started going out and one day I turned up at her place stoned and she noticed at once. She didn't know it was smack or anything but she said straightaway: "What've you taken?" She's a bright lady. I was sort of a bit ashamed so I told her and she said: "If you ever take it again, that's the last time you'll see me. If you want to wreck you own life, that's your problem, but you're not mucking about with mine." I've never touched it again and I got a good job. I don't know but when I'm with her, everything seems possible. We're going to get married next year.'

The role of circumstances is well demonstrated by the fact that 95 per cent of the US troops who used heroin in Vietnam stopped without any treatment as soon as they returned to the US.

It is, perhaps, surprising that heroin is ever given away free. Frequently it is not addicts, whose needs force them to be very miserly with the drug, who offer it to someone for the first time. Rather it is users who have not yet reached the stage of physical addiction, who still believe that they are in control of their drug use, and who consequently do not fully understand the dangers of what they are doing. Yet even addicts sometimes have more than they immediately need. The motives for offering it can be as innocent as wanting someone else to enjoy a pleasure one has discovered, much as one might offer a book one has enjoyed. Equally some users want the reassurance of company in doing something they know they should not. Some. too, enjoy corrupting others, just as some men enjoy deflowering virgins. Whatever the motivation, the act is outrageously irresponsible, but then irresponsibility is one of the key aspects of heroin use.

What follows is the story of how I came to try heroin. It does, I think, illustrate how barriers are weakened and also the role of chance – how, in fact, 'normal' people can come to try heroin. Because it is spread over three years, it is heavily concentrated and contains only what I think is relevant. As such, like all the quotes, it is no more than a personal opinion.

At 15, I was a scholar at one of the top public schools. I wasn't brilliant but I worked hard, because, until then, it had not occurred to me that I had a choice. I had just been confirmed into the Church of England. I had a strong, but intensely personal, faith, bordering on the mystical: worship to me was to be alone in a beautiful building and meditate on the patterned colours of stained glass thrown by the sun onto the white, worn stone floor.

Over the next year my attitudes began to change. I began to realise that I did have choices, that hard work was not the only thing in life. The first major decision I faced was what subjects to take as 'A' levels. My parents thought it was time I started taking my own decisions; they were ready to advise but I was to decide. In this case it was easy enough: I picked the subjects I was best at.

However, a process started then that became more and more acute as I grew up and my choices broadened: I thought far too much. The more I thought about a choice, the less it seemed possible to say that this path rather than that one would lead to my goal. I knew how much was outside my control, how some unexpected event could turn a good choice into a bad one. And the more I thought about my goals in life the less sure of them I was. If I thought I wanted to be rich, I would think of the sacrifices I would have to make and wonder whether, when I looked back at 60, I would think they had been worthwhile. What I needed was to be blinkered and led, not have to make up my own mind. I needed a criterion for life but I didn't have one. I lost faith, because it seemed to me that Christianity's prescriptions were irrelevant or impracticable. I managed to ensure I had no barrier of faith or ambition.

I was, however, scared of drugs in general. In fact, I tried cannabis because I was scared of it. I was with some older school friends during the holidays. They impressed me, because their parents were rich, unlike mine, and they had lots of smart friends. When the joint was passed to me, I was so worried about showing I was scared that I took it. It had no noticeable effect on me, as is often the case with cannabis the first time, but it took away the fear and made the next time seem a far less important decision.

I left school to take my Oxbridge Entrance exams at a tutorial in London. By then I had been smoking cannabis on and off for nearly two years. After the exams I was asked, together with someone on my course, to do some redecorating in the tutorial building. The second day, while we were still shifting furniture about, my co-decorator suggested we take some LSD. I knew as little about it as I had about cannabis before trying it. I only knew one could have a 'bad trip': whatever that was I was sure I didn't want it. He pointed out that he was only going to give me so little that the effect would be no more than that of a joint. So I tried it and, indeed, the effect was indistinguishable from cannabis. Three days later, he suggested we take some more. This time was quite different. I strongly suspect that he intentionally gave me a larger dose, although the strength of LSD is notoriously erratic. I was expecting to be mildly stoned. Instead I felt as if someone was pouring liquid perceptions into my head to drown my mind. I couldn't think for the jumble of tastes, colours and smells. I thought I was going mad.

Almost exactly a year later, I was just down from my first term at university and in the middle of my first serious love affair. I went with my girlfriend to see a fringe play at the ICA in London. I can visualise the scene exactly as we came out at the end, because, in hindsight, so much hinged on those two or three minutes. It was a typical, wet, December night as we walked away and I saw a black car pull off the road, way up by Admiralty Arch and come towards us through the rain. In it were two girls I knew, and the driver whom I'll call David. So much of the next year centred round that meeting with David, yet I can't satisfactorily explain how he came to be there at just the moment we emerged other than by chance. The car was too far away to have been waiting for us and it is very hard to judge just when a play will finish.

We all went back to where my girlfriend was living. David at once asked for a mirror and produced a packet of cocaine. When I was offered a line, I refused: cocaine to me was a hard drug and not to be compared with cannabis. Then, too, I couldn't help thinking of my experience with LSD. I was amazed that my girlfriend accepted. When he saw me refuse, David came over to talk to me. He was in his early thirties and had been a doctor. He was also intelligent and charming. He patiently explained to me that cocaine was popularly portrayed as far more dangerous than it really was, that it was not addictive and that its only damage was to the nasal membrane, which should be washed out from time to time. He didn't persuade me to try any but I liked him.

I discovered over the next two weeks that many of my friends seemed to know David. Yet it was as if he'd appeared from nowhere; no one seemed to know much about him. Then, on Christmas Eve one of the girls who'd been in the car when I'd met him offered me some cocaine that he'd given her. Perhaps because it was Christmas and because so many of my friends, including my girlfriend, had tried it, I thought 'What the hell?' She handed me the packet so, not knowing enough about it, I took too much. I began to sweat profusely; my hands shook and I was chain-smoking. Yet at the same time it made me feel well and happy.

Had I not seen David again, I would probably have rarely, if ever, taken cocaine again, because I certainly couldn't afford to buy it. But David seemed to be following me around. Over the next six months I kept running into him. I came across him in a crowd of 10,000 at a rock concert at Wembley. At Easter I went to Paris to see my girlfriend who was learning French. We went to a party and there was David. Back in London, I was walking along a street at 2 in the morning, when a car pulled up beside me; it was David's.

He had told me to come to his flat any time I liked. So, at the end of my summer term at university, I went straight there. Unfortunately, no one had bothered to tell me that my girlfriend had walked out on me and was living with a Parisian. Nor did I have any idea that she was in England. When I arrived at David's, she was there, with her new boyfriend.

I was miserable and over the next few days I saw a lot of David. He was the one person I felt I could talk to: many of my friends had known about my girlfriend and I couldn't forgive them their silence. Then, of course, there was always cocaine available at David's. The cocaine cheered me, but he cheered me more. He said to me: 'Admit it, you were bored with her. You gave her the chance to go and now you're rid of her. You did it in the nicest possible way.' This wasn't really true, but it boosted my confidence.

The days became weeks and the weeks months and David became a very close friend; I was under his spell. Even after what happened, I still feel that summer was one of the best times of my life. His flat was endlessly full of rock and film stars. There was a non-stop flow of champagne and cocaine. We went out to dinners of caviar; we emerged from nightclubs at 4 in the morning; and we drove down the M4 to see how fast the car would go and to see the sunrise. I never paid for anything and I finally discovered where his money came from. He had given up practising as a doctor when he realised it was more profitable to import cocaine.

He repeatedly told me never to touch heroin. He used to say: 'Everyone thinks they can control heroin but they can't. No one can. Heroin always controls you. It's a fantasy.' One of his favourite expressions was, 'It's a fantasy', and even by the time I met him protracted cocaine use had turned his life into a fantasy. He didn't notice that reality was slipping. He wasn't mad, but nor was he living in the everyday world.

Just before I went back to university, I went to see him. A friend of his had just arrived from Ireland with an ounce of the purest heroin I've ever had. For some reason David decided that I should try some. I refused, pointing out that he had always warned me against it. He argued that one should try everything once. He put out a line. It sat there for six hours, while I obstinately refused his sporadic urgings. Finally I was so stoned on the cocaine that I capitulated.

I didn't take heroin again for another nine months but the damage had already been done. My barriers were down.

Building barriers

Knowledge about heroin is one of the weakest barriers and yet one of the easiest to build. Schoolchildren are taught about sex; they should be taught about drugs – all drugs, from alcohol to solvents to heroin. The same thing is at stake: health. Unfortunately it is one thing to teach; it is another to be believed.

Belief depends upon credibility, and credibility depends upon real knowledge. Ignorance can have disastrous results. A fine example of this is the anti-drug propaganda put out by the US government in the late 1960s and early 1970s. It wildly exaggerated the dangers and damage of cannabis use. When these claims were shown to be false, the government lost credibility so that its valid warnings about drugs such as heroin were ignored.

Belief also depends upon respect. Yet there is increasing disrespect for authority of any kind. The young are often more prepared to respect and believe film and pop stars than parents, teachers or government bodies. This suggests the desirability of using well-informed unsensational films rather than teachers for drug education in schools. The films should preferably involve well-known figures from the entertainment world; there are certainly enough of them who have had first-hand experience of drugs.

It may be the responsibility of the state to educate children about drugs, but it is the responsibility of parents to build other barriers against drugs. William Burroughs said in his seminal book on the subject, *Junkie*: 'You become a narcotics addict because you do not have strong motivations in any other direction. Junk wins by default.' Parents have to encourage those things that provide strong motivations in other directions. This means encouraging their children's interests, however bizarre, however unlikely to lead to a job. It is so important to have an interest or hobby that either demands commitment or provides pleasure.

It also means providing children with a morality, not necessarily the morality of the state but a set of standards by which to live. It is better to start with a set of standards that are below the norm than to find that some have to be discarded later under the pressure of circumstances. To discard one standard is to weaken the whole structure. Children, when they are old enough, need to play a part in deciding this set of standards so that it is not wholly imposed by parents and so they can accept and believe in it. Discipline at home is important because it does encourage self-discipline. A noticeable common factor amongst addicts is a lack of discipline in their childhood.

Parents' attitude to religion often discourages belief among their children. This is unfortunate because religious belief is a wonderful prop. Some people, too, have a definite need for a spiritual aspect to their lives, the lack of which can be very strongly felt but is often hard to identify. The religion does not have to be Christianity. Parents could do much by teaching their children about the major world religions and encouraging a belief of some sort.

Perhaps most important of all is that parents should have the sort of relationship with a child in which the child can come to the parents and say: 'I tried some heroin last night and I'm worried about it.' Frequently people are worried the first time they try heroin but turn not to their parents for guidance but to friends who are taking the drug and who consequently tend to reassure them. It is when someone has taken the drug only once or twice that it is easiest to discourage them from taking it again. Timely intervention can rebuild the barriers. Children are much more likely to come to their parents with their problems if they feel that their parents know something about the problems and can understand them. In this case that means knowing about heroin.

I am aware that this is a prescription for a lot of work for parents, for a deep involvement in the lives of their children. I can speak only from the point of view of the child. Having children is a far greater responsibility than people generally realise. If you are going to bring them into the world, at least prepare them properly for it.

CHAPTER FOUR

Heroin

'The first time I tried smack I loved it. I know most people have reservations and think they'll be careful so they won't get a habit. But I just knew I was going to take it again and again whenever I could.'

Heroin *is* nice. Ignoring the consequences and the problems associated with it, the effect of the drug is pleasurable. It is not pleasurable only for a certain type of person; it is as generally pleasurable as, say, sex. While writing this, I met a woman who works as an administrator in a clinic. She is happily married, has two children, and loves her job. She doesn't smoke, drink, or take drugs of any kind. She certainly has no wish to escape from her life: she enjoys it too much. Six months ago she was admitted to the clinic in considerable pain. While waiting for an operation, one of the nurses gave her an intravenous injection of morphine, which has an almost identical effect to that of heroin, although it is, weight for weight, less strong. She said to the nurse: 'My God, this is wonderful.' The nurse replied: 'Now you understand why young people take drugs.' She told me: 'Yes, I did understand. We've had a few cases of heroin addiction at the clinic and I always used to think how stupid they were. I still think they're stupid, but now I have some idea why.'

That heroin is generally pleasurable is not to say that everyone who tries it likes it the first time. Very often, the dosage is wrong the first time, Whereas a long-time user can tell with extraordinary precision how much he needs, the neophyte is clearly unable to do so. So he has to rely on the giver to judge the amount for him. If the giver has built up any tolerance to the drug, it is virtually impossible for him to remember how much less he once needed or to calculate it by abstraction. The problem is further complicated by the differing strengths of different batches, resulting from imperfections in the manufacturing process and adulteration. It is also true that susceptibility to the drug varies from person to person: like alcohol, heroin tends to have a more pronounced effect on the highly strung.

Thus the first time it is tried the dose will typically be too large. To take too much is not necessarily unpleasant; even a fatal overdose is not, producing an almost instantaneous loss of consciousness. Rather, the strength of the effect and its novelty tend to make considerations of pleasure irrelevant. The first time I tried it, even though I insisted on taking only half of the amount that was offered to me, I cannot say I liked it; but neither did I dislike it. It hit me so strongly that I had to fight to stay conscious, yet I was not at all concerned that I kept verging on the point of blacking out. The drug removed my worries about its own effects.

The most common reason for disliking heroin the first time is that it frequently makes one sick. This can be as much a reaction to the taste of the drug when it is smoked or sniffed as to the drug itself. The feeling of sickness is most srongly experienced in an upright position. Often a user will feel fine after taking the drug, only to have an uncontrollable urge to vomit as soon as he stands up. How unpleasant this sickness feels varies.

'Smack used to make me throw up a lot to begin with. But I never used to mind it. It wasn't like being sick normally, when you feel really yucky. It was more like sneezing, just a sort of convulsion. I didn't feel ill or anything: I just went on feeling stoned.'

Larger doses tend to increase the feeling of sickness. This sickness can be enough to dissuade a first-time user from trying it again.

However, the body adapts quickly and sickness is rarely experienced after the first few times.

It is a minority who like heroin the first time they try it. For the majority, the novelty of the experience must wear off or the dosage be corrected before they can appreciate it. To some extent, it is necessary to learn to like heroin, in the same way that the taste for a new food or drink is acquired. How many coffee drinkers liked coffee the first time they tried it? People typically try heroin a second time for the same reason they tried it the first time, but their resistance to doing so is that much lower because they have aready taken it once. Even those who actively disliked it the first time may try it again.

'The first time I tried it I really didn't like it – it was too strong. It made me throw up and I didn't like getting that out of it. And then afterwards I thought: "You must be mad. That's heroin you're fooling about with. The capital H for trouble." But then a couple of months later I guess I went mad again.'

In time it is easy enough to forget the unpleasantness of the first experience, particularly if one has friends all of whom seem to like the drug. However absurd it may seem that someone who dislikes something should go on taking it until they do like it, especially if that something is bad for them, nevertheless it is an observable phenomenon. How many cigarette smokers coughed violently over their first cigarette and yet continued?

What exactly it is about heroin that appeals varies with each user, his character, his situation. Typically, after the first few times a user will pick on one or two of the drug's effects as his reason for continuing to take it. It is also true that heroin can affect different people differently and the same person differently in different circumstances, although the essential effects remain constant. It is the peripheral effects that vary. To understand what the drug does it is easier to consider its physical and psychological actions separately, even though such a distinction is somewhat arbitrary:

in one sense all the psychological effects are really physical, since they are caused by the introduction of a chemical into the system. The distinction is, however, useful, because it is the physical effects that are ultimately responsible for physical addiction, the route to which is often characterised by a mental addiction. This differs from a physical addiction in that, whereas for a physical addict life without heroin *is* worse, to a mental addict it only *appears* to be worse by comparison.

Physical effects

Although by weight or volume heroin is much stronger than opium and morphine, in equipotent doses it has the same principal effects. Indeed, it was the search for a drug that had the advantages of opium but without its liabilities that led to the introduction first of morphine and then of heroin.

By the beginning of the nineteenth century, addiction to opium, once called God's Own Medicine, had become a major social problem. So, when morphine was isolated in 1803, it was hailed as a major scientific breakthrough. It became freely available, sold over the counter often in the form of patent medicines and was advertised as a cure for opium addiction. Inevitably, opium addicts became morphine addicts.

In 1874, heroin was first reported by an English chemist, but it was not until 1898 that the German pharmaceutical company, Bayer, seeing its possibilities, began to manufacture it commercially. In a remarkable proof that we learn nothing from history, it was greeted as the drug to cure morphine addiction. That the medical profession, following its experience with morphine, could have believed that a drug derived from it and much stronger could have been any less addictive is incredible. As late as 1910, the *Encyclopaedia Britannica* had the following to say: '... morphine is frequently better replaced ... by heroin, which checks irritable coughs without the narcotism [drug addiction] following upon the administration of morphine.' It is hard to believe that they are describing the same drug.

As an analgesic, heroin lowers the body's awareness of pain. In this it differs from an anaesthetic, which blocks either the sending or the reception of the pain message depending on whether it is a local or general anaesthetic. Someone who has taken heroin will still be aware that he has, for example, burnt himself but the burn will hurt much less. As a pain-reliever, it is far more effective than any drug a doctor will usually prescribe. Exceptionally, for headaches it is less effective than the far milder aspirin or paracetamol.

This analgesia is intimately connected with the sensation of euphoria, the feeling of well-being, that heroin engenders. The euphoria, which has both physical and psychological aspects, affects pain by dissipating the anxiety it causes. Not only is pain perceived less acutely; it also loses its importance. It hurts less, because one does not care that it hurts.

'It's that wonderful moment you feel it washing over you. I don't quite know how you'd describe it. It's a sort of pleasurable detachment. You know sometimes how you feel your body too much, as if you've got too much attachment to your surroundings, you're too much aware of your physical self. Well it's a sort of release from that.'

In effect, the mind withdraws from the physical world of the body with its cares and pain. In its cocooned isolation, the mind looks out on the world with detached contentment.

The euphoria is experienced at its most physical when the drug is intravenously injected. Because it is put directly into the bloodstream, its effect is almost instantaneous, jolting the central nervous system.

'The first time, someone did it for me. I couldn't believe how quickly it hit me – I mean the plunger wasn't half in. It just blew me away – so far away, in fact, that I watched the plunger going in the rest of the way as if it was all going into someone else's arm. I didn't seem to be there at all.'

The only way to convey the 'rush' produced by intravenously injected heroin is to compare it to sexual climax. While they are similar in intensity and pleasure, they differ in that, whereas sexual excitement builds to a climax, the 'rush' of heroin transports one immediately from one state to the other. The experience is heightened by the very abruptness of the change. This abruptness is the reason that most long-time addicts take heroin by injection. Whereas the state induced by heroin, if it is experienced enough, can become the 'normal' state and therefore boring, the 'rush' is always pleasurable. For the same reason, when tolerance has built to such an extent that an addict can no longer get enough heroin into a syringe to give him a 'rush', cocaine, which provides an equally abrupt jolt to the central nervous system, is often mixed with it.

An important component of heroin euphoria is its relaxant action.

'It's like, you know, when you come in from a hard day chopping wood or whatever – that moment when you sit down absolutely knackered. Only it's better. You feel it flooding through your body, sweeping away the aches and tiredness and tenseness. Magic.'

Just as the body can be too tensed up, so can the mind. This is most apparent, because it is most annoying, at night. Sometimes it is impossible to get to sleep because the mind keeps on turning. Heroin slows the mental process. In a society where tension is so pervasive that, via high blood pressure, it accounts for a significant number of premature deaths, relaxation has become an art. How much simpler and preferable it can seem to take a chemical, as the number of tranquillisers handed out by doctors shows. Heroin also slows reaction time, making it advisable to avoid activities, such as driving, that may require rapid responses.

Overall, heroin slows down the body's activities: the heart rate slackens and the respiratory system is depressed. It is this respiratory depression that causes death in cases of overdose. This is characterised by loss of consciousness and increasingly shallow breathing until breathing stops altogether and there is a bluish tinge to the pallor of the face. At the first sign of an overdose, the person should be taken to hospital. Other users are often unwilling to summon an ambulance, because an overdose will be reported to the police. In that case, private transport or a taxi should be used. Overdose symptoms, however, usually appear quickly because overdoses are typically taken by injection. If breathing has already ceased, artificial respiration must be applied at once and, if the heart has stopped, attempts must be made to restart it.

'This son-of-a-bitch turned blue on me. I don't take the muck myself so I wasn't used to people ODing on me. I hadn't the faintest idea what to do but I was buggered if I was going to let him die on me. I started slapping his face to try and bring him round and then I realised his heart had stopped. I thumped it but I couldn't hear anything so in desperation I stuck two of his fingers into an electric socket. And he came round. Thank God!'

True heroin overdoses are rare. Most cases that appear to be overdoses are due, not to too much heroin, but either to some existing condition such as heart or liver trouble or, more frequently, to adulterants in the heroin. There is generally enough time to get the person to hospital.

Heroin also inhibits bodily secretions. So it makes urination and ejaculation difficult and is constipatory. It is very effective in removing the symptoms of colds by drying up the nose and eyes and suppressing coughs. However, by lowering the metabolism, it hinders the body's ability to fight the germ. Heroin can also lead to temporary sterility and play havoc with menstrual timing.

Additionally, it causes irritation of the skin: users are very often seen scratching.

After a large dose, a user will often begin 'nodding'; that is, his head will loll forward and he will drift into a state similar to dream-filled sleep. However, in this state, he has more control than in a dream over the thought images that pass through his mind, since they are the product of his conscious rather than his subconscious.

> 'The thing I love about gear is nodding out. You just sit there and let all those pictures wander through your head. Then you come to with a start and then drift off again. Of course I can never remember afterwards what went through my head.'

Heroin causes a degree of amnesia. It is extremely difficult to remember what one has done on heroin. Heroin time differs from usual time, because, in retrospect, it barely exists, if at all. Like the time spent sleeping, it is time out of life. What remains in the memory is the moment of pleasure when the drug first enters the bloodstream. As a narcotic, it allows a very deep and prolonged sleep.

Extreme long-term usage causes the teeth and hair to fall out, but, in general, heroin is far less damaging than is usually supposed. The drug itself comes low down on the list of most harmful substances – below, for example, amphetamines, cocaine, tobacco and alcohol. The physical problems of heroin use are caused not by the drug but by the lifestyle associated with it and by the way it is taken. Injection is the main culprit here, although there may be serious problems connected with smoking it. Certainly asthma sufferers find that smoking heroin dramatically increases the difficulty they have in breathing.

Psychological effects

The psychological effects are, in many respects, analogous to the physical. Just as heroin cocoons the mind from pain, so it does from the cares and anxieties of life.

'After my father died I carried round with me this awful guilt, because the last time I'd seen him we'd parted on really bad terms. Then I discovered smack. Smack gave me the detachment to see how stupid my guilt was, because I couldn't do anything about the past, and indeed how unimportant my father's death was, how unimportant all life ultimately is. By reasoning this out when I was stoned and free from my normal emotional overload, I found I could carry this reasoning over into the time I wasn't taking smack. It helped me a lot.'

The euphoria of heroin is a very effective anti-depressant.

By slowing down the mind, it prevents that crowding in of anxieties that makes rational thought and hence solutions so difficult. When financial, work and emotional pressures arrive simultaneously, it is often hard to separate them and confront them individually. Heroin removes the pressure of the problems. However, it also tends to minimise them and thus also removes the pressure for solutions. It is therefore far more useful for problems for which the passage of time is the only solution, such as the death of someone close.

Heroin's ability to push problems out to arm's length until they seem simplistically soluble is a part of its general self-confidence inspiring action.

'I used to get pushed around a lot by some of my friends, because I was shy and not at all sure of myself. And they used to tease me in front of girls, which used to really embarrass me. Once I started taking smack, I wouldn't stand for it any more and I couldn't be embarrassed by anything. I had to watch it though, because I knew it was making me very argumentative. I kept catching myself on the point of defending myself when I knew I was in the wrong.'

Depending on the personality or the mood of the user, this confidence can be exaggerated into an overbearing arrogance and aggressiveness. The drug acts then as a stimulant rather than a depressant. I remember an occasion when this feeling took hold of me while I was driving. I began to drive with outrageous aggression, running red lights and screaming abuse out of the window at anyone who got in my way. I was spoiling for a fight.

For the user this feeling is marvellous: he is Caesar with the world at his feet. For others it can be insufferable. I once went into a small shop run by a Pakistani with a white English friend who was in this frame of mind. He bought some chocolate and, then, without warning began this one-sided conversation with the shop-keeper: 'Over here for long, are you? Come on a banana boat, did you? Like it here then? Better than where you come from, here, is it? No mud huts here – you must feel out of place. Not staying too long, I hope. Well, goodbye. Have a good trip home. Soon.'

Similarly, although heroin is a relaxant, it can make users very short-tempered and irritable. Occasionally it is because the user resents any intrusion on the inner tranquillity that the drug has given him. Usually, however, it is only an aspect of the egocentricity of the drug: no one has the right to approach Caesar without Caesar's permission.

Heroin dispells boredom, particularly if it is used infrequently. In part, this is because the heroin state of consciousness differs from the normal. The change itself is enough. But it acts in other ways too. For example, the boredom generated by doing something in which one has no interest, say shopping, is lessened: while standing in the queue at a check-out counter, heroin allows the mind to wander euphorically elsewhere. The boredom or repetition is lessened by the amnesia the drug causes, because the awareness and memory of the preceding identical actions are lessened. Time on heroin is almost exclusively present time: the future seems far away and unimportant and the past fades rapidly from mind.

'My boyfriend takes heroin. I try and discourage him, but I do not understand why he does it. He's got such a high IQ that he's supposed to be regularly monitored at Cambridge. He's a genius really. He doesn't have enough stimulation so he gets bored. Not just ordinarily bored like you or me, but desperately bored and that makes him really depressed. His doctor explained it to me. His mind's like one of those motors that, if they don't have a load, just go spinning faster and faster until they burn themselves out.'

Curiously, this slowing down of the mind makes it enjoyable to read or watch television or a film. It is curious because the heroin-induced amnesia makes it very difficult to remember what has happened so far and, therefore, to know what significance the present action has. I've watched someone reading an Agatha Christie book. Each time he got to the end of the page, I interrupted him and chatted for a couple of minutes. He would then go back to the same page, look at it, not recognise any of it and begin to read it again. He cannot possibly have known who had murdered whom or, indeed, who any of the characters were. Yet, when I asked him, he told me that he thought it was a great book.

It is hardly an exaggeration to say that heroin has something to offer everyone.

'Smack is the ultimate escape and who the hell doesn't have something they'd like to get away from? The trouble is that it keeps finding more and more things you want to escape from. And you end up trying to escape from escaping.'

The adantages of heroin are undeniable. So, too, are its liabilities.

Towards addiction

Heroin is addictive. This does not mean that everyone who tries it will become addicted. Some discontinue use before they have truly decided they like it. A few are able to avoid addiction by rigidly confining their heroin use to certain specific occasions, such as one weekend per month. Such ritual use tends to avoid many of the problems associated with drug use of any kind. Alcohol, too, is addictive but it is those who stick to rituals such as only drinking with meals who avoid alcoholism. Unfortunately, heroin is much more addictive than alcohol.

If someone takes heroin day after day, no matter how he takes it, he will inevitably become addicted. How long it takes depends on the frequency of dose, its size and purity. Because of these variables there is no general rule. However, between one and two months of daily usage may be taken as a rough guide and two weeks of very heavy daily usage as a minimum. However long it takes, there are no exceptions and, surely, almost everyone who tries heroin is aware of at least that one fact about it. So why do users go on taking it until they do become addicted?

It is too simplistic to explain it in terms of addictive personalities. And it is quite untrue to say that users have a subconscious wish to become addicted. It is inconceivable that any sane person would want to be an addict. Users continue to take the drug in spite of, not because of, its addictive nature.

Some users are under the mistaken impression that heroin is only addictive if it is injected. It is possible to argue that heroin is more addictive when injected in the sense that more of a given amount will enter the bloodstream if it is injected than if the same amount is taken any other way. But it is wholly wrong to believe that heroin use is in some way not dangerous or serious simply because the heroin is 'only' sniffed or smoked.

For some it is simply a question of carelessness: they pay no attention to the number of days they have taken it without a break.

'My boyfriend was dealing so it was there and it was free so I took it and went on taking it. It sounds pretty dumb, doesn't it? But I just didn't think about getting a habit. My boyfriend had one but it didn't matter, because he always had stuff.'

It can be very difficult, without experiencing it, to understand what it means to be addicted, to envisage the feeling of heroin deprivation. If one does not understand addiction, it is easy to minimise its importance, easy not to bother to think about it.

Some users are aware of the seriousness of addiction and, yet, refuse to think about it. This attitude of taking pleasure on the never-never was typified by my brother.

'The only excuse I can give is that I was young. I was only 16. I never thought about consequences – I'd make myself sick on chocolate cake. I took smack whenever I could because I liked it. It was as simple as that. Finally I took it often enough to get a habit.'

Those who drift into addiction characteristically think of heroin taking simply as a pleasurable experience and do not examine what precisely it is about the drug that appeals to them.

Others are fully aware of where their heroin use is leading but continue nevertheless. Often they begin taking it on certain, specific occasions so that it becomes associated with those occasions.

'I had this mate. He used to live on the same street but he moved away. But we tried to get together pretty regularly. We got into the habit of going to see a flick together once a week. He used to bring his bird who'd got him into gear and he used to give me some. I never took it but when I went to the flicks with him. One week they didn't show so I went in alone. Half way through the picture I walked out because it was crap. It took me a while to figure out that I thought the film was rubbish cos I hadn't had any gear.'

Without the drug, the occasions seem to lose something to become dull and pedestrian.

This is more than the association of a cigarette with a cup of coffee that smokers find it so hard to break. It is more comparable to the feeling of someone who goes back to an uninteresting job after a wonderful annual holiday. At first the job seems worse than usual, because he sees it in contrast to the holiday. The difference is that for him the feeling does not last long because he knows that he cannot go on holiday again for another year. The heroin user, however, knows that he can easily recapture that feeling. It requires perhaps as little as a phone call, £10 and a couple of wasted hours. Its very facility exacerbates the temptation.

'I'd been invited to this party and I really wanted to go. The last few parties I'd been to, someone had always given me some smack – I knew quite a lot of people who were taking it at the time. It made all the difference: it – I don't know – kind of brought me out of myself, I suppose, stopped me feeling shy. Anyway I got to thinking about this party. I kept thinking: 'It'll be so much better if I take some smack.' I knew I couldn't rely on being given some. So if I wanted to be sure I'd have to go and score some before. I knew what a dangerous thought pattern this was but I just couldn't get out of it – my mind kept harping on it. I finally decided I wouldn't go unless I got some, because I knew, just knew, that I'd hate it if I didn't have any. So then I proceeded to convince myself of all the reasons I *had* to go: I'd promised to go; a girl I rather fancied was going to be there you know the sort of thing. So I went and scored. And I remember knowing in the back of my mind that that was it – by giving in that time I wasn't going to be able to say no again. Yet I shut my mind to it.'

The user finds more and more occasions that would be better on heroin until life itself seems increasingly dull without it. He finds that certain events are not merely better on the drug but cannot be faced without it: a visit to the bank manager, a job interview, a meal with his parents. Each time he surrenders to the temptation this feeling increases so that the next time it is harder to resist. Even his increasingly brief glimpses of the trap into which he is walking serve, perversely, not to strengthen his resolve to resist but to weaken it: he wants the escapism of heroin to forget what he is doing.

The user is now psychologically addicted. Life without the drug is perceived as worse than it was before he tried heroin: there are mental deprivation symptoms. Although not all users are psychologically addicted before they become physically addicted, all physical addicts are psychologically addicted. It is this that makes a full cure so difficult. Once discovered, it is impossible, ever, to forget how nice heroin is.

A user aware that he is psychologically addicted will typically attempt to fight it by making rules for himself. I did it myself: I decided to have a two-day break for every two days I took it consecutively. Such rules are far easier to make than to keep. There is always some special, overwhelming reason to take it on one of the days off. Each extra time is just an 'exception'. The rule disintegrates.

The increasing desire for heroin inevitably puts the user under financial pressure.

'I had a job at the time and every time I got home at the end of the day I'd think: 'What shall I do tonight?' when there was only one thing I really wanted to do. The only reason that I didn't have a habit was that my dealer would only sell between 5 and 7 in the evening and often I wasn't home in time. But I was still spending more than I could afford. I'd think to myself: "Oh, well, it'll be all right at the end of the month when I get paid", as if somehow, magically, next month I would suddenly stop wanting to buy smack. Yet I knew it wouldn't be like that but I refused to think beyond the end of the month. I deliberately cut short my horizon, as if I could make everything afterwards disappear. Then things really started getting out of hand. I was too scared to open the letters from the bank; I had to avoid people I'd borrowed money from; and I was into my dealer for quite a lot. I couldn't see a way out. I was taking smack to forget the mess taking it had got me into. When I found I had a habit I thought I'd just taken the one irreversible step. But, of course, that had happened long, long before.'

Users sometimes claim financial pressure as the reason for switching to injection as the method of administration. Since the effect of heroin depends on how much reaches the bloodstream, and since by the other methods some of the drug is absorbed by the tissue and so does not reach the bloodstream, injection makes financial sense in the short term. Over the long term, for a given amount of heroin, it makes no sense: tolerance builds more quickly and, hence, the need for larger doses and more money.

In reality, users switch to injection because of the 'rush'. That they feel the need to find some other justification for doing so is an indication of the view, even among users, that injecting heroin is much more serious than sniffing or smoking it, that it characterises a 'junkie' rather than someone who is in control of the drug and only takes it from time to time.

Most users, like most people, start with a horror of needles. Typically, curiosity or the reassurance of other users that it will not hurt overcomes the initial reluctance. Users generally learn how to do it by watching others and often have someone else do it for them the first few times.

'My brother persuaded me to try it. The first time I couldn't even bear to watch. I just held out my arm and let him get on with it. It was amazing. I knew that was the way I wanted to take it. I got him to do it whenever I wanted some. It didn't hurt at all, because he always used new needles and blew on the spot where he was going to put the needle. And he always hit the vein first go. Then, one day when I wanted a hit he was out. I was kind of afraid of doing it myself, but then I thought, what the hell And it was easy.'

So often users are shocked the first time they experience the symptoms of heroin deprivation. Typically, they have either conditioned themselves to believe that it is they who are in control of the drug and not vice versa or they have avoided facing the inevitable conclusion of their actions by thinking in discrete segments: it is easy, seeing the spectre of approaching addiction, to begin to think: 'This next bit won't get me addicted.' This is the equivalent of thinking that this one cigarette will not cause cancer. Although these statements may be true in isolation, they are clearly fallacious when applied to a continuing series of cigarettes or heroin doses. Addiction is thus a shock and its symptoms often ascribed to some ordinary illness.

'That first time, you wake up and you think you've got "flu" only you don't remember feeling this twitchy with "flu". And then you realise. You've got a habit. You can't pretend any longer. Now you know all that stuff about 'Oh, I can handle smack' was just so much bullshit. And you were the only sucker that believed it.'

CHAPTER FIVE
Addiction

'Smack starts off as a carrot; but it ends up as a stick.'

Without heroin an addict will be ill. That is the meaning of addiction. How ill he will be depends on the size, in terms of accustomed daily dosage, and the length of the addiction. No longer is it simply that the addict wants the drug to get 'high'; he needs it just to function normally. The fear of heroin illness is the ultimate motivation for an addict to continue using.

Some addicts certainly have a fear of heroin deprivation out of all proportion to the severity of the illness itself. Such fears have been magnified by certain sensational films that have depicted heroin deprivation as a truly horrific experience. Doctors, on the other hand, tend to think that it is no worse than flu because the symptoms are, physically, similar to a bout of flu of varying severity. The truth lies somewhere between the two extremes. What doctors tend to ignore is that suffering is essentially mental, not physical. Not only is heroin deprivation unpleasant and painful; it also raises the body's sensitivity to pain to an acute pitch, thereby magnifying the unpleasantness of the physical symptoms. Added to this is the addict's ever-present knowledge of the instant cure. Some addicts, too, base their fear of deprivation on their own experiences of being without the drug. They *know* what it is like.

Because heroin is needed by the addict, it tends to take first place in his list of priorities. Although a few can retain a measure of control over their addiction, for most addicts it narrows down existence to a cycle of raising money, buying the drug and taking it. It is a way of life. The time required to raise the money and buy the drug leaves little or none for any other aspect of life. So it becomes almost impossible to hold down a job, to have friends, to do anything that is not connected with heroin. 'Normal' life disintegrates.

> 'When I didn't have a habit, if someone was pissing me around, I'd just tell them to forget it and not score. There's only so much hassle you can put up with. But when you're a junkie, you've got to put up with the hassle. So you spend about a quarter of the time getting stoned and the other three-quarters trying to. Jesus what a life.'

The size of an addiction is determined by money. In general, an addict never has enough money. The more he has, the more heroin he can buy and take per day, the more his tolerance builds and, so, the more he needs to take and the more money he needs. And, the greater his daily dosage, the iller he will feel without it and, so, the greater his drive will be to get it. Health tends to suffer, because food takes second place. Morality is so often discarded because it is too expensive. Crime becomes almost inevitable.

Most addicts encounter despair at some point. It becomes clear that heroin is no longer permitting an escape from problems; it is creating them and they are becoming increasingly difficult to solve.

> 'Taking H is like digging a hole for yourself. The more you dig, the deeper you get. The only way out is the way you came in. The deeper you go, the harder it is to climb out.'

Some think they are in too deep ever to get out and, seeing the pointlessness of what they are doing, take an intentional overdose. Others try to stop but, because they try it on their own, almost always fail. Rarely will an addict ask for help. It involves admitting too much.

Deprivation

Continual heroin use causes the body to react in two ways. It decreases production of a series of substances known collectively as endorphins and it raises the metabolic rate to compensate for the depressant action of heroin. These reactions occur progressively, allowing the body to tolerate the effects of increasingly large doses as well as to break down, or detoxify, those doses more quickly. Conversely, when the drug is withdrawn, it takes time for the body to readjust. This is the cause of the deprivation symptoms.

Endorphins, which are chemically similar to heroin, although up to two hundred times as strong, are produced by certain glands in tiny amounts. They appear to have the same effect as heroin and, thus, continual heroin use makes them unnecessary and so slows and finally halts their production. Like heroin, their primary action is analgesic, although, paradoxically, pain is not the main stimulus for their secretion. They are the cause of the pain associated with heroin deprivation. Their absence is typically experienced as aches in the back and legs. And in general, just as heroin lowers the awareness of pain, so its absence accentuates that awareness.

Since endorphin research is far from complete, it is as yet unknown how many of the other deprivation symptoms are due to their deficiency. The other cause of heroin illness is the body's attempt to raise its level of activity to compensate for heroin. The more that heroin depresses the system, the harder the body works to raise its rate to the normal level. Consequently, when heroin is withdrawn, the body is fighting a no longer present enemy. Until it readjusts, it is in overdrive. It works as if the addict were running a marathon, even when he is sitting down.

So, deprivation is characterized by a high heart rate and a simultaneous feeling of extreme physical edginess and exhaustion.

'Quite apart from feeling sick, you feel so hyped up you can't sit still. Yet at the same time you're so knackered you don't feel as if you've got the energy to do anything and, anyway, you don't want to do anything. Or, rather, there's only one thing you want to do.'

There is a frequent need to urinate and a twitchiness in the joints as if they are being jerked by invisible threads. Stabbing stomach pains are common, sometimes so painful that an addict has to bend over double to obtain some relief. As with flu, the nose and eyes run and there are alternate bouts of sweating and shivering. Nausea is often experienced, particularly in the mornings. Male addicts have an overwhelming and entirely physical sexual urge manifested in a hair-trigger climax.

Like the body, the mind is in overdrive, turning over and over on itself. This, together with the physical edginess, makes sleep at night very light and broken, if possible at all. However, the exhaustion of a continually overworking body will often make an addict drop off for a few minutes during the day.

'It was hell. I kept tossing and turning all night. I just couldn't get comfortable. My legs especially couldn't keep still. Finally I'd doze off for a bit and then come to, absolutely freezing. So I'd pile on more blankets and then start sweating. And that smack sweat smells so awful. It's as if the body's getting rid of something rotting. And I'd keep having to get up to have a pee. I'd have got up and done something if there'd been anything I could've faced doing and if I hadn't felt so tired. Then, next day, whenever I tried to concentrate on anything, I'd get this wave of sleep. I'd close my eyes and get these colours and geometric patterns dancing round my head like a visual image of all my cells jumping around with excess adrenalin.'

In the same way that deprivation increases physical sensitivity, it also produces a severe emotional vulnerability, coupled with anxiety and a loss of self-confidence. Boredom is usual, in that the racing mind makes it almost impossible to concentrate and destroys both the interest and the drive to do anything.

Deprivation sometimes causes an intense depression. Because this is of chemical rather than emotional origin, it is impossible to think oneself out of. I went through it a few times, but not every time I was without heroin. It made me feel as if a veil had been drawn between me and the world, through which passed words and events of rational meaning but of no relevance to me. Everything outside me existed only on a factual level; there was no human understanding or compassion, no emotional connection. I have never been so intensely conscious of my own isolation.

Perhaps the worst suffering caused by deprivation is the result of knowing that heroin, the cure to the sickness, is there, if only some way can be found to obtain it.

'You tell yourself that you know you can't get any but you can't help thinking about it all the same. Just thinking 'if only' winds you up so much more than you would be normally. You go on and on thinking until you find a way that you think just might work. And suddenly you're so excited. You see the possibility of release from the agony. So you go out and do whatever you have to do to get it.'

It is this way in which an addict's mind works that so often drives him to commit crimes. The mind harps on the subject, which both makes the suffering worse and minimises the difficulty or immorality of the action necessary to find the money to buy heroin. It is, therefore, a generally accepted fact that heroin illness is significantly more bearable when the addict knows he cannot get any heroin.

Deprivation symptoms set in a few hours after the effects of the last dose can no longer be felt. How long this is depends on the size of the dose and the addict's tolerance. However, typically, if the last dose is taken before going to bed, the symptoms will become apparent the next morning. They reach a peak on the second day and mostly disappear, or are greatly reduced in severity, by the fifth day. A somewhat higher than normal metabolic rate and an inability to sleep may, however, persist for some time.

Disintegration

Heroin addiction is a way of life because of the time it requires. Just buying heroin always seems to take longer than one thinks it will. Because it is illegal, the supply is never certain and, because most of the people involved in selling it use the drug themselves, they are unreliable.

'Even after you've got the money together you ring some guy who tells you to ring back in an hour. And when you do he tells you to ring back in another hour. Meanwhile you're getting sicker by the minute. So finally you ring someone else who says he knows where to get some. So you meet him in some pub and he goes off with your cash, saying he'll be back in half an hour. Two hours later he's still not back and it's closing time. So you hang about in the cold outside 'cos you don't know where else to go, sure by now he's done a runner. But he's got all your cash and you're sick, so you wait. Finally, he turns up stoned out of his mind, probably on your gear, and says: "Sorry, man, but you know how it is." You just want to kill assholes like that.'

The necessity of time-keeping makes it almost impossible for an addict to hold a job.

'As soon as I got home from work I'd try and score. But often it took hours so I wouldn't get any till about 11 p.m. Then I'd stay up taking it till 1 or 2 a.m. Often I just crashed out in a chair and woke up at 7 in the morning still in the clothes I was going to have to wear to work again in an hour. Several times I'd get to bed so late or so stoned that even an alarm call wouldn't wake me. I'd come to about mid-day and think: "O God, *Work*.

What can I tell them this time?" I think finally my grandmother had died just once too often and they threw me out.'

To lose a job is to lose a source of income, which, therefore, makes it all the more difficult to support an addiction.

Yet it is possible to have both an addiction and a job. I had both for almost two years. Indeed, I had a habit when I went for the first interview. It was a question of priorities. The job, at least for a while, was more important to me than heroin: if necessary, I was prepared to feel ill at work. Even when I had enough, I would resist the temptation to get 'stoned' at work and take only as much as I needed to avoid feeling ill. I was sent on a five-week accountancy course, which took place at an English seaside resort, in January. That, of course, is the reason we were there: the hotel was offering very cheap rates. I decided that five weeks away from London would allow me to give up heroin. For the first four days I felt awful and the town was cold, bleak and depressing. By the Friday I was beginning to feel almost human again. Then I discovered we were allowed the weekends off. So I went home to London and spent the weekend taking heroin. By Sunday night my habit was back so that the next week was as bad as the first. Next weekend I was home again and so this continued for five weeks. The stupidity is almost unimaginable. On the other hand, to get through the days and mitigate the heroin illness I concentrated as hard as possible on the course with the result that I came top of it.

I should stress that I was able to keep a job and a heroin habit only because I was lucky. Firstly, my addiction was comparatively small and, because I was prepared to put up with feeling ill from time to time, it stayed small. Secondly, for much of the time I was living with my brother who was also addicted. As he was not working, he had time to waste buying the drug. Thirdly, I had the motivation. However, when I lost the motivation, when I became bored with the job and it lost its importance relative to heroin, then my life did fall apart.

Partly as a result of heroin amnesia and partly because of his altered priorities, an addict will neglect the bills he had to pay, the things he has promised to do, everything, in fact, that is unconnected with heroin.

'If I was invited to stay with someone for, say, a weekend, I had to make sure first that I had enough smack. If I said I'd go on Friday night but couldn't score, I simply wouldn't go. My behaviour was erratic to say the least.'

Friendship, love, anything that requires giving, cost too much in terms of time for an addict.

Morality, too, is too expensive and inconvenient for an addict. In almost every case addiction demands lies and theft at least. It is a measure of the success of heroin as a teacher of deception that the lies of addicts are so frequently believed.

'I had a habit and I was living with my Mum and she found out all about it. I stopped for a while and then I started taking it again here and there. I was real careful not to act the way she thought a junkie does, you know, nodding out, sleeping late, and not caring shit about anything. So, even when she found a works, she believed when I said it was left over from the last time. And I was stoned when she asked me. 'Course I had some mates who'd gone straight too and they knew straightaway I was using again. You can't fool a junkie about being stoned.'

An addict learns to lie as a matter of course. He lies to his dealer about the money he is going to receive tomorrow in order to get credit today. He lies to explain his peculiar behaviour to people who have no connection with heroin. He lies about the top-quality heroin he knows where to buy so as to persuade other users to give him their money.

There is no honour among junkies as there is supposed to be among thieves. A junkie is alone and everyone to him is a target to be cheated, robbed and deceived.

'I can't believe now the things I did and, before I got the smack, I would never have believed I would ever do those things, no matter what the pressure. What I said was more often untrue than true. If I was scoring for someone I'd take as much out of what I'd got for them as I thought I could get away with. I ripped off masses of people. At one point I had a dealer who was very untogether. I once managed to nick twenty quid from him, score a quarter and then persuade him I'd already paid, so I came out with the smack and money. Another time he nodded out while I was there so I took about a gram out of a bag he'd stupidly left lying around. Next day he rang me and said: 'You really shouldn't have gone without waking me last night, because if something had gone missing I'd have thought it was you." So I said: 'Well, it was lucky then, wasn't it?"'

Friendship among addicts is based on need not on trust, because one cannot trust an addict, or rely on one. Your problems are never their problems.

Addicts are more often immoral than amoral. They know that they are being driven to do things they should not. Yet this is frequently a spur to take the drug. They want the drug so as to be able to forget what wanting it has made them do.

Health as well as morality has to take second place to heroin. Food costs money that could be spent on heroin; it is a bore to prepare; and it takes time. In addition, heroin considerably reduces the feeling of hunger. But it also lowers resistance to disease, although at the same time minimising the unpleasantness of any symptoms.

Most health problems associated with heroin, however, are caused by intravenous injection. Death is the major, although a comparatively uncommon, hazard. Overdosing, in the proper sense of taking too large a dose, is rare. It typically occurs to one-time addicts who have stopped for a while and not taken into consideration how much their tolerance has fallen during that time. More common are the deaths from blood clots, the poor condition of the liver or adulterants mixed with the heroin. Injected air bubbles, on the other hand, have to be much bigger than is generally assumed to kill.

The veins form a delicate, closed system that should be interfered with only under clinically sterile conditions.

'I was round scoring at my dealer's and he asked me if I wanted a hit there. I had my works with me so I said OK. He gave me this spoon. I can't tell you, man – it was *black*. On the inside, not the outside. Maybe it was smack it was coated with, but it could've been anything. I said to him: "What've you got in here man, a zoo?" cos I thought I saw something jump out of it. He couldn't understand what I was talking about. "It's just the spoon I always use," he said. So I said: "Sure, but don't you ever clean it?" he looked sort of blank and said: "What would I want to clean it for?" So I said: "Well, do you think I could use another?" I'd've offered to clean his but I didn't want to spend the rest of the night there.'

Addicts are generally too careless or in too much of a hurry (because they are feeling the effects of deprivation) to take adequate precautions against infection. Consequently, abscesses and diseases like hepatitis are common. Even a tiny piece of dirt can cause what is known as a 'dirty fix', which results in violent bouts of shivering, so violent that it is impossible, for example, to drive. After a few hours in bed, however, the effects pass.

'We'd just scored and we were both dying for a hit so we went into this Gents' and, of course, the tap over the basin was fucked. So we went into these cubicles side by side and I took the top off the cistern and got some water out of there – I had everything else, works, spoon, lemon, tie, with me – and had a hit. And wow the relief. It sounds masochistic, but a hit is so much better when you're sick than when you're straight. Anyway we came out and I said to him: "I had a hell of a job getting that cistern top off." He looked at me as if I were nuts. I said: "You did take the water out of the cistern, didn't you?" No, he'd taken it out of the *bowl*. Can you credit it? I couldn't decide if he was suicidal or just plain dumb.'

The problem centres, however, around syringes. Quite apart from the overuse of a single vein, which causes it to sink and finally collapse, 'disposable' syringes, the type in general use amongst addicts, are supposed to be used once only. Re-use blunts the needle points and sloppy handling can barb them, both of which damage the veins more than is necessary.

'I always use a new set of works every time. It's really short-sighted not to. You've got to look after your veins or they start becoming very difficult to hit and then you have all sorts of problems. I once flew down from Glasgow with someone who had three hits on the flight. Can you imagine what would have happened if we'd hit turbulence while he was doing it?'

Syringes are usually only washed out with water between uses, an obvious potential source of infection. Much more dangerous is when one addict borrows the syringe that another has used. I have even watched a boy share an injection with his girlfriend. That is, he injected himself with half of what was in the syringe and then gave it, still containing the blood he had drawn into it to check that he had hit the vein, to his girlfriend to finish. It is hard to think of a more effective way of transferring disease.

Most chemists will not sell a syringe to anyone who, in one pharmacist's words, 'looks as though he wants it for an illicit purpose'. Some, however, do sell syringes, knowing full well the use to which they will be put. They reason that, if people are going to inject themselves, it is far better that they should do so with new sterile syringes. At present there is no law against selling syringes; it is at the discretion of each chemist.

This is, I think, the worst possible situation – syringes are easy enough to obtain if one wants to, but hard enough to discourage anyone who has an old but serviceable one. If syringes were available from every chemist, it is probable that the incidence of heroin-related disease would fall. It might also be, however, that the proportion of users taking the drug by injection rather than another method would rise. Like heroin itself, the use of syringes is dependent to a large extent on availability. The more freely available syringes are, the more likely that a user will come into contact with them and perhaps begin injecting.

Conversely, were the sale of syringes to be outlawed except on prescription, injection might become less common. When a user begins injecting, he is typically much more careful about the use of new syringes, because he can always return to his previous method of administration. Only after a period of injecting does any other method of administration seem almost unthinkable.

If the sale of syringes were to be made illegal, some rise in the incidence of disease amongst addicts already habituated to injection may occur, but on the other hand, the difficulty of obtaining syringes may force some of them to seek treatment. In the long run this could possibly reduce the health hazards associated with heroin use.

Money

Even on Customs' estimates, over 3 million grams of heroin came into the country last year. At an average price of £80 a gram this represents around £250 million spent on heroin last year. This is a minimum figure, because it takes no account of adulteration, of short measures or of the practice of selling it not by weight but in packets worth £5 or £10. This money had to come from somewhere.

Raising money is an addict's primary problem. A habit of half a gram a day requires a minimum of £40 every day or almost £15,000 a year.

'I used to wake up every morning and wonder where the hell I was going to find the money to score today, let alone to buy food or cigarettes or anything else. Mind you I almost always found a way. It's amazing how inventive the threat of feeling sick makes you.'

When an addict has exhausted the legal ways of raising money, such as borrowing or selling his possessions, he is forced into crime.

Theft is the most common heroin-related crime. Often it begins at home, not because the addict has anything against the people he lives with, but because it is easier. Outside the home, shoplifting is the commonest form of theft.

'I used to go shoplifting every day just about, mostly clothes. At least with shoplifting it's not too bad if you're nicked. I tried to lift things I knew my dealer would swap for gear, because it's such a bummer having to sell things and anyway you get such a lousy price. He moaned a bit but he mostly took the things, partly because he quite fancied me. I hated shoplifting when I was strung out because it made me so paranoid. But then when I was stoned I couldn't be bothered. At one point I *had* to do it stoned because I had such a bad habit that being sick immobilised me.'

A considerable amount of house-breaking is heroin related and also fraud, particularly with stolen chequebooks and credit cards. There is, too, a small amount of prostitution.

'I never went out on the streets. God, no. But I did ask this friend of my father's to lend me some money. When I went to get it, he wouldn't let me have it unless I went to bed with him. I needed the money because I had a habit and so ...'

Britain is, as yet, remarkably free of heroin-related murders. In Spain, for example, several Britons have recently been killed or wounded and handbags snatched for the money to buy heroin.

Another way of raising money is to go to a doctor who will prescribe saleable drugs. The drug problem in Britain in the 1960s and to some extent in the 1970s was largely due to over-prescription by doctors. The Brain Committee reported that in 1962 one doctor alone prescribed 600,000 heroin tablets. Prescription of pharmaceutical heroin is today tightly controlled, although it still finds it way onto the streets. Other drugs are more in evidence.

'I know this doctor. For £15 he'll write a script for 30 Diconal. As I can flog them for a fiver each, that's quite a good deal.'

There is a proper street market in the Piccadilly area of London. It is fed largely by the over-prescription that still continues amongst private doctors, who make fortunes from this practice. Typically part of a prescription is sold to pay for the next one. Drugs such as Diconal, Palfium and Methodone that can be found there are heroin substitutes and are sometimes preferred to heroin. Diconal, for example, the brand name for dipipanone, is a pink pill designed to be taken orally but it is often crushed, dissolved and injected. I think it gives a better, more intense 'rush' than heroin.

'I remember the first time I scored at the 'Dilly. I was looking for dry amps [ampoules of pharmaceutical heroin]. I went up to several guys but they only had rit [Ritalin, a type of amphetamine] or wets [Methodone ampoules]. Then I saw this tall guy. He said he had some. I told him I wanted two. All the time we were walking up Shaftesbury Avenue in the middle of the afternoon. Well actually I was more like running 'cos this guy took such fucking great steps. So he says: "Give me the bread." So I'm getting the thirty quid ready as coolly as I can and then he sees some guy across the street and then he waves and shouts, "Do you want something?" I'm shitting myself. I mean this ain't some deserted bit of country. Half London are walking past. Anyway I give him the bread and he stops and gives me the amps all open like as if I was buying a paper or something. Fucking freak out. I needed the scag after that I can tell you.'

Even Methodone, which, when injected, gives no 'rush' at all, can be sold and the proceeds used to buy heroin. There is always someone who wants it in order to break their heroin addiction without going to a doctor.

Perhaps the most obvious way of supporting a heroin addiction is by dealing. Very often this is not a conscious decision but rather something an addict drifts into.

'I had this really good contact. He was dealing really excellent dope and I was the only one who knew him. So quite a lot of people started asking me to score for them. In the end I was scoring between 1 and 2 grams a night for other people so I said to this guy: "Look, why don't you lay, say, 5 grams on me so I don't have to come and see you so often." That suited him because you don't want too many people coming round all the time or people notice and that's how you get busted. So that's how I started dealing properly.'

When I was taking heroin, I met someone who was selling it in bulk. I began buying a quarter of an ounce at a time. As this cost £250, the equivalent of about £35 a gram, I could have made money dealing. I didn't because I was working and so did not have the time. Almost every addict at some point buys for others, which amounts, at least legally, to dealing. Conversely, addicts hate having someone else buy for them because the buyer will almost inevitably take some of their heroin as commission. It pays to cut out middlemen.

The need to turn to crime for money inevitably increases the risk of contact with the police. Inventive as addicts may be, they tend to underestimate the risks they run or to become careless. I walked unwittingly into a police raid on my dealer's house because I failed to notice that a huge plate-glass window beside the door had been smashed. The police had jumped through it with guns drawn. They had cleared it up considerably before I arrived but there was still glass all over the pavement. I had been too careless to notice.

The police are not by and large sympathetic to addicts. It is not their job to be. They do not have the time and, besides, they are fighting a battle against drug abuse, a battle they are losing.

'There may be more unpleasant places to have cold turkey than in a police cell but I can't think of one. Police cells aren't exactly the Ritz when you're feeling well, but when you're wondering if you can make it through the next minute ... Well it's my definition of Hell. I just sat there with my knees against my chest rocking backwards and forwards, resigned to my agony. The police refused to give me any medicine, although they'd promised they would – after all I did turn myself in. All they gave me was a blanket, which is about the same as giving a starving man a single cornflake.'

Trying to stop

Addiction is an awful way of life. Most addicts realise this at some point. Addiction leads nowhere; the 'money–score–fix' cycle just turns on a static axis day after day. With the concentration on heroin and the consequent disintegratioin of everything else there remains less and less of normal life to cling to. It becomes increasingly impossible to hold on to the illusion that a way out is just round the corner.

An addict has, by definition, lost control of his body to the drug. Yet the events on which he relies so much are also largely outside his control.

'There are always days when everything goes wrong. And it always seemed to me that the worse my habit was, the more

likely things were to go wrong, as if life was out to get me. I
can't count the times I couldn't score and had to wait in cars or
pubs while someone tried their last-ditch contact. I remember so
often praying: "God, please let him have some, just this once.
Then I swear I'll stop tomorrow." As if God would trust a
junkie to stick to a deal like that!'

Faced with the apparent randomness of his life, an addict, not
surprisingly, can feel helpless and hopeless.

Heroin can become more than the centre of an addict's life; it
can become everything. I have watched addicts probing again and
again with the needle for an elusive vein, tears of increasing
desperation in their eyes, as if their existence itself depended on
getting the heroin into their bodies. I have myself burst into tears
when I pulled the plunger out of the bottom of the syringe and my
last bit of heroin ran out onto the carpet.

Addicts unable to find heroin will often inject themselves with
anything they think will have an effect, such as tranquillisers or
sleeping pills. Part of this is undoubtedy due to 'needle fixation', a
mental addiction to the idea of injection.

'When I couldn't score I shot up vodka. I wanted to get stoned
but I also wanted to have a fix; otherwise I'd just have drunk the
vodka. Actually shooting it gives quite a good buzz.'

I have even watched someone inject themselves with pure water: he
wanted so badly the feeling of a needle in his arm.

Addicts are especially prone to desperation in the state of
emotional vulnerability caused by heroin deprivation. It is easy in
such a state to be overwhelmed by guilt, to see no way out or
anyone to turn to.

'There was no one I could talk to. I couldn't go to my parents.
They wouldn't have understood and they'd have been horrified
and outraged. And I didn't dare tell my junkie friends how

scared and desperate I was. I thought they'd just think I was weak.'

I remember sitting at a table, in front of me an open packet of heroin containing, I reckoned, enough to kill myself. I tried to think of a single reason not to do so. I couldn't.

Giving up heroin by oneself is extremely difficult. Many addicts try. Almost all fail. Part of the reason is that giving up looks so much easier when one is 'stoned'. This underestimation of the problem results in a failure to prepare oneself properly.

'I didn't have a very big habit but I'd been taking smack for quite a while and – I know it sounds unlikely – but I was bored with it. Being stoned had become my normal state of mind. So I decided to stop. I had enough pills and things so I didn't feel too dreadful physically. I stuck it out for two days. By then getting stoned had stopped seeming boring. It was the one thing I wanted to do.'

To deal with physical addiction, addicts sometimes try a reduction cure. This consists of buying a certain amount of heroin and dividing it into packets, one for each day, each with a bit less than the last. This does not work. Anyone with the willpower necessary to stick to this system is far too strong-minded ever to have become addicted. There is always some good reason to dip into the next day's packet. Each extra dose is an exception until ten days' worth of packets has gone in three.

Alternatively, addicts buy drugs to ease withdrawal symptoms or go to a doctor for them. Some fear going to a doctor because doctors are required by law to notify the Home Office if they are treating anyone addicted to heroin. The notification is, however, for statistical purposes and appears never to have been abused. Theoretically, the police do not have access to the notification list, although they have been known to get the names of those being prescribed controlled drugs from chemists. Many doctors, too, refuse to prescribe the most effective drugs for withdrawal and hand out only mild pain-killers, tranquillisers and sleeping pills, which provide little relief for a heavy addiction.

Even with something as effective as Methodone, giving up is very hard. Typically addicts try to do it at home, surrounded by friends who are still taking heroin.

'It's quite amazing. Whenever I tried to stop, someone would ring me up and say: "I've got some great gear. Do you want to try some?" Or someone would come over and *give* me some – someone who was normally as tight as could be with smack.'

I experienced exactly this phenomenon when I tried to give up. It is as if addicts dislike the idea of one of their number giving up.

The more important cause of failure is the inability of addicts to tackle, without help, the underlying reasons for their heroin taking. Truly, physical addiction is only a small part of the problem. Its removal is, by itself, rarely enough. And the more often an addict tries to give up and fails, the more he comes to believe he will never succeed and the deeper he sinks into despair.

CHAPTER SIX

Recognition

Heroin is a problem that rarely goes away of its own accord. It is the nation-wide failure to recognise and face the problem that has resulted in its enormous expansion and the paucity of facilities to deal with it. Ignoring heroin use is not far short of countenancing it. This is particularly true if the user lives with you. In general, the longer that heroin use continues, the more destruction it does to the user and the harder it is for him to pick up the pieces again afterwards. It is no favour to a user to ignore his heroin taking whether you are a parent, a spouse, a lover or simply a friend.

More than this, if you refuse to recognise or to admit to yourself that someone you know is using heroin, particularly if the user is a member of your family and living with you, you lay yourself open to exploitation. You also lay yourself open to the financial and emotional destruction an addict can wreak in those around him.

Although obvious signs of heroin taking should not be ignored, equally, a single possible sign should not be taken as conclusive evidence. There is sometimes a tendency, because the subject is heroin and therefore unknown and frightening, to panic and jump to quite erroneous conclusions. It is rare to find something as obvious as a syringe, which clearly requires immediate discussion, because the injection of anything is extremely dangerous. Rather, the signs tend to be either difficult to spot or open to other explanations. This chapter is intended to open your eyes, not to start you on a witch hunt.

If you suspect someone of using heroin, accusation is not the best approach. Whether he is using or not, faced with an accusation, he will almost certainly not admit to it and he will be put on the defensive. It is extremely hard to help someone who is on the defensive. It should be discussed but, assuming you want to help, it should be discussed as unemotionally as possible. It is best to explain calmly the things you have noticed that have led you to suspect heroin taking and to offer help. There is, of course, no guarantee that a user will admit to it. You can, however, show that you know something about the problem and that you are prepared to help and thereby lay the groundwork for him to come to you at some later point. You can also keep your eyes open for further signs. And you can take precautions.

There are three types of signs of heroin taking. The most unequivocal are the objects used to administer the drug. Injection, particularly, requires a number of utensils. Heroin also has visible physical effects on a user and, over the long term, it can cause quite dramatic changes in someone's physical appearance. Finally, a user's behaviour changes. These are perhaps the most difficult signs to pin on heroin. In that case they can be treated as problems in their own right. So, if you live with someone who is out late every night, oversleeps and is late for work, you can treat this as a behavioural problem and, for example, suggest that he limits his nights out to two per week. If heroin is the cause, such action will typically bring it out into the open.

Objects

Heroin is a white or brown powder. It is much less crystaline than sugar and almost as fine and fluffy as flour. Its most characteristic feature is its intensely bitter taste. It is generally contained in special packets in amounts of up to 1 gram. These are made of paper, preferably of a thick non-absorbent type to prevent the heroin sticking to it. The pages of glossy magazines, for example, are often used.

Heroin is sniffed in the same way as cocaine. Generally a piece of glass such as a mirror is placed flat. The heroin is laid out in thin, straight lines, more for presentation than any reason. A razor blade is ususually used to do this, although, whereas cocaine has to be chopped into a finer powder with the razor blade, heroin is already fine enough. A piece of paper, often a banknote, is then rolled into a tube thin enough to fit into a nostril. By bending back a corner of the outside end of the paper, the tube can be made to remain rolled up. Straws are also often used as tubes. When the drug is sniffed through the tube a tiny amount of powder catches on the side of the tube. Traces of powder also tend to remain on the glass off which it was sniffed. In both instances, a dampened fingertip run along the surface will pick up the powder. If it tastes very bitter, it is almost certainly heroin. If it is mildly bitter and numbs the tongue slightly, it is cocaine.

When heroin is smoked, it is placed on a piece of aluminium foil and heated from beneath with a match or lighter. The heroin then melts and runs along the foil giving off smoke which is inhaled through a tube held in the mouth. Kitchen foil is the type most often used.

'I don't like that cooking foil. It's too thick so you have to heat it so much that the smack burns too quickly and you don't get so much out of it. Much better's that chewing gum wrapping foil. You have to burn off the backing paper first to leave just the foil. It's really thin so you need a really low heat. The best thing is to tear off a strip from a tissue and roll and stretch it so it looks like a piece of string and light that. It burns very slowly and very low.'

As heroin is melted and runs up and down a piece of foil, it leaves easily identifiable dark (or black if it has been heavily adulterated) tracks behind it on the foil. Cocaine, which can also be smoked in the same way if it is turned from a chloride into a sulphate with ammonia in a process known as 'free-basing', leaves only the faintest, very light tracks. The underside of the foil is generally blackened by the heat used to melt the heroin.

The tube used for inhaling the smoke, like that used for sniffing, can be made of anything. Typically, however, it is also made from aluminium foil and is about three inches long. It is often crimped two or three times along its length. This limits the interior size of the tube and forces some of the smoke to resolidify into heroin. The tube can then be unrolled and this heroin smoked. Users do this because they think they get more from their heroin in this way.

Since it is the most complicated method of administration, injection requires the most equipment. The heroin has to be dissolved, for which a dessert-size spoon is usually used. One mother said to me: 'If I'd bothered to count the kitchen spoons, I probably wouldn't have had to worry about the silver ones.' Heroin and water are placed in the spoon and heated. Heat is generally insufficient to dissolve brown heroin and some form of mild acid must be added such as a few drops of lemon juice or vinegar or citric acid or vitamin C powder. A small piece of cotton wool or cigarette filter is used to filter out any bits of dirt or undissolved adulterants and the solution is drawn through this into the syringe.

A tourniquet such as a tie, a belt, a dressing-gown cord, even a piece of string, is then tied above the vein to be used. So, for example, if one of the veins in the crook of the arm is chosen, the tourniquet would be tied around the biceps and the arm pumped up and down from the elbow. This forces the veins to stand out. The needle is slid into the vein, the plunger pulled back to draw a little blood into the syringe to check that the needle is in the vein and the solution pushed into the vein.

'Hitting the vein's a knack. It's a sort of feel, but you don't feel it in the vein. You feel it with the hand that's holding the works. If the spike's not sharp, you can sometimes feel a pop as it goes in. Really you just sort of get to know the depth and the angle. Like anything, it's just practise.'

Injection can be very difficult. Some people have tiny veins or veins that naturally lie deep beneath the skin. Difficulties are exacerbated by habitual injection, which forces the veins to sink and hardens and scars them. A vein is a small target. It is easy to miss it, or to go right through it, or to hit it and then to have the needle slip out again when the tourniquet is removed or during the process of pushing in the plunger.

Not surprisingly, injection can be very messy. It gets messier with each failed attempt to hit a vein. Each failure tends to make an addict more desperate, less calm and, so, more likely to fail again.

'My hands were shaking so much because I was so strung out I nearly knocked over the spoon when I was cooking it up. Then I hit the vein and it came out. So I had to start again while the first hole kept pumping out blood. Then I couldn't hit a vein or I went through it. I was messing about so long that the blood in the works clotted and blocked the needle so I had to get it all out into the spoon again and use another works. Blood all over the place. What a mess.'

Blood very often gets onto whatever is used as a tourniquet and onto clothes. Even when an injection is successful first time, when the syringe is withdrawn some blood spills out from the punctured vein. If this is not properly staunched, it can stain clothes. As veins in the arm are most commonly used, shirt sleeves are the most frequently stained.

Users are unlikely to leave the implements for taking heroin in some visible place. If they do, it may well be a plea for help. Also, the implements are not necessarily kept together. It would be unusual to find a mirror with a rolled tube and razor blade on it. Typically, you come across things by mistake: you find some scrunched-up foil while emptying a wastepaper basket or a packet while emptying pockets before putting a pair of jeans into the washing machine.

The implements can be hidden anywhere. However, packets of

heroin are very often kept in wallets or in the back of cigarette packets. Foil tubes for smoking heroin are also kept in cigarette packets because they are about the same size as cigarettes. Because water is necessary both to dissolve the heroin and to clean out syringes, the implements for injection may be stored in the bathroom. Bathrooms are also private and so ideal for the act of injection. Addicts usually keep the small balls of cotton wool through which the heroin solution is drawn into the syringe. Because some of the heroin always remains in these balls, they can be boiled up, when heroin is unavailable, to provide some relief from heroin sickness. These balls are often kept in matchboxes.

Ordinary household objects can only suggest heroin taking if they are found in unusual places. A lemon, a packet of kitchen foil or a spoon mean nothing in a kitchen. They may mean something in a bedroom or bathroom. Spoons tend to bear clear evidence because users rarely clean them. When it is dissolved, impure heroin leaves a deposit on the inside of the spoon and the heating blackens the underside and so anything the spoon is put down on such as a carpet or a table. It is worth knowing that a spoon's blackened bottom can be effectively cleaned with a damp piece of kitchen paper dipped in cigarette ash.

Physical appearances

When heroin enters the bloodstream, it causes one immediate, physical change: the pupils of the eyes contract – to the size of pinpoints, after a large dose hence the slang expression 'pinned', meaning under the influence of the drug. The pupils naturally contract in bright light and expand in dim light. Consequently it is almost impossible to tell from the pupil size if someone is 'pinned' in bright sunlight, but comparatively easy inside, in artificial light. Pupil size is easier to spot in those with blue eyes rather than brown because the black of the pupils stands out better against blue. Heroin also dries up the eyes' lubricating liquid. This emphasizes

the whites of the eyes, giving them a luminous look, and is again
more noticeable in blue eyes.

Heroin contracts the pupils because it depresses the body's level
of activity. Cocaine and amphetamines, on the other hand, are
stimulants and so expand the pupils. So, when they are taken with
heroin, the opposite effects are cancelled out, leaving the pupils of
normal size. Similarly, because an addict deprived of heroin is
overstimulated, his pupils will be unnaturally expanded.

Smoking and sniffing heroin rarely leave physical traces.
Occasionally, when heroin is sniffed, some powder may remain
around the outside of the nostril and sometimes, when it is
smoked, some heroin resolidifies into a shiny brown gum on the
teeth. In contrast, injection always leaves marks. A single injection
produces a small pink bump that disappears after a few days. A
series of injections typically follows a straight line along a vein,
known as a 'track'. A 'track' turns purple before disappearing.
However, serious overuse of a vein causes scars that can take a very
long time to disappear. Even after three years of not injecting, the
scars in the crook of each of my arms are still clearly visible. They
are, in fact, so bad that they are not easily recognisable as heroin
'tracks'.

Heroin takes the colour from the face, making it appear pallid.
The lifestyle associated with continual heroin use, in which food
and health take second place, tends to make this pallor permanent.
For the same reasons, continual heroin use is typified by weight
loss. This causes the cheeks to sink and, together with the pallor,
can drastically alter a user's facial appearance. These changes are
most dramatic and visible if you have not seen the user for a while.

'You're not going to believe me but I swear this is true. The
mother of a girl I know was walking down the King's Road. She
saw someone she thought looked vaguely familiar so she crossed
over to talk to them. It took her three or four minutes to realise
it was her daughter.'

Hepatitis is one of the most common diseases amongst users who inject themselves. It turns the whites of the eyes, and eventually the skin of the face itself, yellow. Because it is a liver disease it has to be treated with a very restrictive diet, and the longer it is left untreated, the more damage it does to the liver.

It is not easy to spot the physical effects of heroin. The pallor of someone who has just taken heroin makes him look ill, and the eyes look 'odd'. However, once you have seen someone who you know has just taken some heroin, then it is not hard to recognise again. That is why one addict can spot another, even though he has never seen him before.

Behaviour

The behavioural signs of heroin taking are perhaps the most nebulous, the most difficult to pin on heroin, because they are so open to other explanations. Behavioural changes are easier to spot the more time you spend with a user and the better you know him. On the other hand, some changes, such as a change of friends, come about gradually and so proximity can obscure them.

The narcotic effect of heroin makes users appear to go to sleep, to 'nod out'. This may not seem so odd at 11 in the evening. It should seem odd at 11 in the morning.

'I went with my boyfriend to dinner with his parents. Before we went I had a little smoke to keep myself together. He had a hit. When I saw how much he was putting in the spoon, I said; "Charlie, you can't take that much. Your parents'll see you're stoned." He said: "It's all right. I know how much I can handle. And whose fucking parents are they, anyway?" So, of course, during dinner his eyelids start dropping further and further. I kept kicking him under the table to try and wake him up. I felt I had to say *something* to his parents so I said the first thing that came into my head, which was that Charlie had come off his bike and hurt his shoulder and the doctor had given him some really strong pain-killers. Not only did his parents believe me, they kept saying how lucky he was to have someone like me to look after him, which was a joke, considering it was me that introduced him to smack.'

In the same way, users sleep for much longer than usual and find it hard to wake in the morning. Conversely, an addict deprived of heroin will find it difficult to sleep at all at night and will be fidgety during the day. So, unusually heavy sleeping indicates use; heavy sleeping varying with an inability to sleep, addiction.

Heroin irritates the skin: one of the characteristics of someone who has just taken a large dose is, in addition to drooping eyelids, a lethargic scratching all over the body. Heroin also often makes people irritable and serious. One does not laugh on heroin. It cocoons one not only from pain but equally from what is funny.

'Smack's not a drug for laughter. Your mind doesn't go fast enough to laugh. You have to be pretty up and alert to catch the funny side of the world. That's why dope or booze make you laugh when they act as stimulants. When they act as physical depressants, then you don't laugh. That's also why sometimes when you're coming off you get the giggles. It's not that coming off's funny; it's just that you're so up.'

Addicts have to explain the times they are sick with heroin deprivation. The commonest explanations are, not unnaturally, diseases with comparable symptoms such as cold or flu. A chill often explains a 'dirty fix'. If forced to see a doctor, an addict will emphasize the symptoms that fit and not mention the others; it is extraordinarily easy to lead doctors to the conclusion one wants to hear. An addict may, of course, want to see a doctor if he thinks he can get a prescription for something to relieve his sickness. It is not the 'illnesses' themselves that hint at heroin addiction, but rather their abnormal frequency.

The more that someone becomes involved with heroin, the more he will tend to disregard anything unconnected with the drug. This is especially true of friends.

'I noticed David seemed to have changed his friends. I said to him: "What's happened to Joe?" or "Don't you see Karen any more?" and he'd just shrug and say something like, "Oh, you know, Mum" or "I see them sometimes". I used to really like most of his friends. Instead, he started seeing people who looked shifty to me. He wouldn't introduce them to me if he could help it, which he'd always done before. And he stopped coming to talk to me. He always used to do that, like when I was doing the ironing or something. He'd come and chat and tell me what he was doing at college, that sort of thing. All I got from him now was "I'm going out now, Mum". It was as if a wall had come down between us."

It is also common for those living with a user to receive telephone calls, often late at night, from people who will not leave a name.

Heroin has developed a slang of its own. This serves not only to set users apart from everyone else, but also to make it more difficult for anyone not part of the heroin world to understand what is being discussed. Part of the purpose of the quotes in this book is to habituate readers to this private language. However, when users think there is a real likelihood of being overheard, such as on the telephone, they frequently use even more obscure language or words that are capable of a quite innocent interpretation.

'Whenever I rang my dealer, I'd say: "Can I come over and see you?" meaning "I want to score". He'd ask me how long I wanted to stay, meaning how much did I want to buy. An hour meant a gram; so quarter of an hour meant quarter of a gram. Pretty simple really, but I've heard people using the most incredible codes.'

Perhaps the simplest code is the substitution of a proper name. So, Henry or Harry refers to heroin and Charles or Charlie to cocaine in sentences such as: 'Have you seen Henry?' or 'Is Henry round with you?'

The time and the odd hours that heroin requires should be obvious to anyone who lives with a user. Addicts, in particular, are often late for appointments or miss them altogether, because the appointments are, quite simply, not as important as heroin.

'We went up to London for the day. I didn't have a habit but I really wanted to score. I invented some things I had to do so my parents lent me the car when we got there. I had to meet them an hour and a half later at a restaurant for lunch. So I thought I'd go up to Piccadilly and try there. I was looking for a dry amp but I met this guy who said he could get some proper smack. He told me it was just down the road. It took half an hour to get there. Then the guy said he'd only be five minutes. He was in the house for another half an hour. Then he wanted to have a hit in the car and so I had one too. Of course he couldn't find a vein. I was already late for lunch but the guy kept whining: "Oh, man, just hang on. I'll get one in a minute." In the end I couldn't stand it any longer. It was winding me up too much watching him missing and missing and the time getting later and later and wondering what I could tell my parents. So I drove off. I was driving like a maniac because of the time, while this guy was still trying to get a vein. He'd made such a mess of his arm and there was claret pissing all over the car. Anyway I threw him out when we got back to Piccadilly and cleaned up the car as much as I could. Then I had an idea. I stuck my penknife into the spare tyre. By the time I got to the restaurant my parents had already finished lunch. I told them I'd had a puncture and had had a hell of a time changing the wheel because the nuts were done up so tight.'

The above is a good example of the sort of explanation a user will produce. Indeed, if anything it is rather banal. The problem for users, and addicts in particular, is that there are so many things that require explanation – dubious friends, strange telephone calls, going out at odd hours and being late. The explanations are often inventive: their frequency demands it. There is a limit to the number of punctures one can credibly have in a week. They can sometimes be exotic because the prime requirement is that they should be unverifiable. This is frequently unnecessary because, however exotic and unlikely the explanation, it is so often accepted by a user's family and friends. They would rather accept it than believe that it may be hiding some other, sinister activity. Indeed, it is not so much the unlikely nature of an explanation that should alert you but the frequency of such explanations.

There is a general difference in behaviour in someone when they are taking heroin and when they are not. Except after a large dose, a user remains capable of coherent, rational thought. It is rather his attitude that changes. Because the drug distances him from his surroundings, he tends to be less aware of other people's feelings and needs. He therefore tends to be less kind, less thoughtful and helpful, less tolerant, and in conversation more dogmatic and argumentative. If the user is your lover, the first sign you notice may be a diminution in sex.

If you live with an addict, it is likely that you will notice that certain things go missing. It is not necessarily that the addict wants to steal them from you: he would ask to borrow them, but he cannot risk that you might refuse. The things to watch for are kitchen foil, lemons, pills (especially tranquillisers, sleeping pills and pain-killers), and, of course, money and easily saleable objects.

It is very often difficult to prove that an addict is responsible for a theft. An addict will try to disguise it so that it appears that someone else did it.

'My Mum, went off to stay the night with her sister so I took the tele and the hi-fi – I would've taken the brand-new cooker my Mum had just bought, only I couldn't lift it – and flogged them.

The I went off and scored and didn't get back till about 4 a.m. On my way in I bust a window round the back. My mum was coming back in the morning; so I was planning on getting up early, "discovering" that we'd been "burgled" and calling the cops. Only it being scag, I didn't wake up and it was my Mum that came back and called the cops. The bummer was she didn't come and look for me first. It was like around noon, so I guess she thought I'd gone out. Anyway, when she did come into my room it was with a copper and there was a packet of scag beside the bed. So I got busted for that. But they never knew it was me that nicked the tele and stuff.'

If you suspect someone of stealing money or valuables, it is important not to jump to the conclusion that heroin, or indeed any drug, is the cause. People take money instead of asking for it for any number of reasons. It is better to treat it as a problem in isolation but at the same time to bear in mind that heroin might be involved and to watch for other signs.

Really, any behavioural problem needs to be discussed. It is quite wrong to assume that just because drugs may be involved you are no longer qualified to tackle it. Drugs are not a subject that should be off-limits to everyone but specialists. Drug abuse is too widespread and the number of specialists too small for that. Specialist help is unquestionably useful. First, however, you have to tackle the visible problems, to try to bring the heroin taking, if it is there, out into the open. Then is the time to look for outside help.

CHAPTER SEVEN
Help

Heroin taking often comes to light because of a crisis. The user takes an overdose, or is arrested, or loses a job. Such crises are typically the result of addiction rather than occasional use and can, in the short run, be beneficial by giving the addict the motivation to give up heroin. In the long run, they can make a cure more difficult: it is that much harder to pick up the pieces of one's life after addiction, if one has, for example, a criminal record. It is for just this reason that it is important to recognise the signs of heroin taking and to take some action before a crisis is reached.

Occasional use is, in some respects, more difficult to deal with than addiction. It is harder to recognise: you have a much better chance of noticing signs that are repeated day after day than those that occur only once every two weeks. It is also harder to find sufficient reasons to persuade the occasional user to discontinue his drug taking. It is impossible to argue convincingly that heroin is bad for him if you either drink or smoke at all yourself, since heroin is less physically damaging than tobacco or alcohol. Heroin is, of course, illegal. However, it is hard to rebut the argument that the law has no right to regulate the state of mind of the individual, provided that it does not interfere with the well-being of others, which occasional use need not. The best argument against occasional use, because it is the real danger, is that it is likely to degenerate eventually into addiction. This may not be persuasive, however because in general users are aware that heroin is addictive, but most believe that, despite the experience of others, they are capable of so regulating their heroin use that they can avoid addiction.

That it may be difficult to argue successfully against occasional use does not mean that it should not be discussed or that you have to tolerate it. It is potentially dangerous and it should be talked about. If a dialogue on the subject can be started, it may be possible to monitor the situation, to know if, for example, the use becomes more frequent. It may then be possible to drive home the message that addiction is a real threat. It may also open the way for the user to come to you for help if he does lose control of his use. At the same time, it is best to make clear your own position so that there is no possibility that the user thinks that you approve. So, if you live with the user, you can forbid heroin taking in the house. To permit it is, after all, a criminal offence. If you do not live with him, you can refuse to see him when he is taking the drug. This is sensible anyway, because most people 'stoned' on heroin make dull, if not intolerable, company.

If you are dealing with an addict rather than an occasional user, you face two, or sometimes three, problems. The first of these, the physical addiction itself, is the easiest to solve. It is also the least important. It is quite wrong to assume it is the only problem and that as soon as the addict no longer needs the drug his difficulties are over. It is just this assumption by addicts themselves that is so often responsible for their failure to stop by themselves. It is not enough to stop needing heroin. An addict has to stop wanting it. As Keith Richard of The Rolling Stones put it: 'Giving up is easy. I do it all the time.'

The second problem is the psychological addiction. Although it is not true that every addict is psychologically addicted before becoming physically addicted, none the less all those physically addicted are also psychologically addicted. This is the result of the change in perspective that physical addiction causes. The need for heroin turns it into such a central feature of the addict's life that its removal leaves a void. Think of a priest who suddenly discovers that God does not exist. That is the position of an addict who gives up heroin. However hellish addiction may be, heroin is what an addict bases his life around. Without it there is a gaping hole.

Something has to be found to fill that hole.

Sometimes it is enough to free an addict from the clutches of heroin and give him the time and the help to sort himself out. Time spent talking heroin is time out of life. An addict's existence lacks the change and choice so necessary for maturity. It is an abnegation of responsibility instead of the increasing assumption of responsibility that is so essential a part of growing up. One comes out of addiction at the same mental age at which one entered it. So, in the months following stopping heroin, an ex-addict sometimes catches up the wasted time and, from his new, or mature standpoint, sees how stupid he has been. This can provide him with the motivation to stay off heroin and rebuild his life.

Sometimes, however, there is a third problem: the hole that the removal of heroin leaves in an addict's life cannot be filled because it existed before he ever encountered the drug. This may be the result of a severe psychological disturbance, of which heroin taking is only a symptom. The treatment of addiction *per se* will not, then, solve the problem. Alternatively, it may be the result of social and economic conditions that offer no chance of enjoyment, no hope of improvement, that are only bearable with heroin. For thousands of years man has used drugs to provide relief from otherwise intolerable conditions. It may be that some people *need* drugs. In such a case no cure will work: if someone decides that he cannot face life without heroin, he will go back to taking it. However, that is not a decision that can reasonably be taken while still in the thrall of addiction, because addiction does not allow a straight perspective. For this reason withdrawal from heroin is always worth attempting.

Curing heroin addiction is a formidable, but not an impossible task. Professional help exists, not only for the addict, but for you as well: helping someone through addiction can be emotionally shattering, particularly if there are relapses. Your help is needed. Your participation is not over as soon as professional help becomes involved. At the least, the support of family and friends is vital to prevent relapses when the addict leaves the care of the professionals. Much more may be required because, unfortunately, there are so few professional facilities currently available in Britain. You may also have to make the first moves towards treatment.

First steps

It is very rare that an addict will go to someone close – a parent, a friend, a lover or a spouse – and say: 'I'm addicted to heroin. Please help me.' The subject is still regarded as taboo. Only now is heroin addiction beginning slowly, very slowly, to be demystified. And this is not because people have decided to adopt a saner attitude to it, but because it has reached epidemic proportions. It is becoming commonplace.

While it remains taboo, addicts will continue to be reluctant to admit to it. In addition, it may mean admitting to other things like theft. An addict who asks for help is naturally vulnerable and therefore scared of the response. Will you understand or will you be outraged? The addict's perception of the answer to this question will depend on the relationship between you. But he may also ask himself whether you know anything about heroin addiction and, if not, whether you are able to do anything to help him. It is, therefore, important to answer these questions the first time you mention the subject, whether it has been forced out by a crisis or is still only a suspicion. You need to show that you do know about heroin and that you are willing to help. The aim should be to create an atmosphere in which the addict feels he can talk freely to you.

There is little point talking to someone who has just taken some heroin. The chemical confidence that the drug instils is not conducive to a reasonable, realistic discussion. It is also better to avoid talking to someone who is suffering from the symptoms of deprivation when his view of his situation is chemically altered in the opposite direction and his emotions raw. Is therefore a good idea to ask the addict to come to talk to you when he is 'straight' –

neither 'stoned' nor 'sick'. If he can pick the time, it is unlikely that he will come to see you 'sick', but he may feel that he cannot face such a discussion without some heroin. The best way to tell, aside from the physical signs, is from the tone of his conversation. If he is overly aggressive or defensive, he is probably under the influence of the drug.

If he is 'straight', he may well feel vulnerable, even guilty. The admission of anything can be difficult. How much worse, then, to admit that one has lost control of one's life to a powder. It may be tempting to take advantage of this vulnerability, particularly if you also feel guilty, and hit out. This is almost always a mistake.

'When my Mum and Dad found out I was a junkie, we had this conversation. Well, it wasn't much of a conversation really, because all I said was: "I'm sorry. I'm sorry" over and over, though I was crying so much maybe they didn't hear. Anyway they just went right on about "after all we've done for you, how could you do this to us? You've ruined your father's standing in the neighbourhood and I won't dare show my face round here. We'll have to move you know." And I thought, "Oh, Christ, I've ruined everything, not just my life, but theirs too." I couldn't stand it any longer so I ran out of the house. When I'd stopped crying – I was just kind of wandering about the streets trying to get myself together – I suddenly thought: "Wait a minute. I'm trying to come clean with them and they're laying all this shit on me. They don't really give a toss about me. It's just themselves they're thinking about." So I said to myself: "Well fuck them." And I never went home again.'

It is so much better to show an addict how to make amends than to exploit his vulnerability. The more miserable that you make him, the more he will be tempted to seek the solace of heroin.

That the addict is 'straight' when he talks to you is a good sign. It is a sign of cooperation. For, however much help you are prepared to give, it is worthless unless the addict *wants* to give up heroin. You have to try to establish whether this willingness exists; without it, a cure is very unlikely to be successful. The difficulty is that, if you ask the addict whether he wants to stop, he will almost certainly say yes. This may be true, or it may just be the answer he thinks you expect or it may seem the best option open to him at that particular time. Really, his willingness has to be be gauged from his attitude. If he tells you of the other times he has tried to stop, that is a pointer in the right direction. So too is a realisation of the hopelessness of his situation and a sense of his own responsibility for that situation. It is hard to judge whether an addict truly wants to stop. In the end you will probably be forced to take a chance on it.

It must be remembered that an addict's willingness to stop tends to vary in strength. His motivation may lose its force as he moves through a cure and the pressure of addiction lessens. This why your continuous support is so vital. The offer to help an addict is a heavy, long-term commitment. If you only want to help in a vague, half-hearted way, it is best not to bother – Every failure to stop makes the next attempt that much more difficult. Also, if you are half-hearted, your attitude will probably communicate itself to the addict. That can only be a disservice to him.

You have to think about your own willingness as well as his. If you are both prepared to make the commitment, then is the time to look for professional help, for you both if necessary.

Professional help

It is best to start with your local GP. Even though treatment for heroin addiction is really outside his scope, he should know what services are available. Also the addict may need a referral from him to make use of those services. Then, too, the injection of heroin is physically damaging. Indeed, however it is taken, it can mask the symptoms of unrelated diseases. I had a friend who was taking so much heroin that he did not realise that he had a brain tumour. It killed him. A physical check-up is therefore a good idea, with particular attention, if the drug has been injected, to the veins used and to the liver.

You may find, especially if you live in a rural area, that your GP knows nothing about heroin and that no one in the practice does. Your GP may not admit that he knows nothing about heroin. If you ask him what treatment facilities are available, his ability to answer should tell you whether he does or not. You may feel that he ought to know and, if he does not, feel tempted to criticise him. You should remember that he may still have to provide a referral. More worryingly, you may find that there is such a scarcity of other facilities in your area that you are forced to rely on him for medical help.

You therefore want your GP to be on your side. Unfortunately, some GPs do not want to help, on the grounds that addiction is self-inflicted. Yet they would not refuse to help a smoker with cancer. They seem to dislike the idea that the addict has got so much pleasure from taking heroin. If you wish to change your GP your Community Health Council will help. However, this disapproval can often be mitigated if you go with the addict to see the GP so that he can see that by helping the addict he is helping you.

Indeed, the more that you are involved, the better. There may be a choice of treatments available and the addict may not have a sufficiently balanced outlook for such decisions. This is not to say that you should take the choice away from the addict. He needs to begin assuming responsibility for his life and that should include the choice of treatment, but it may have to be tempered by your commonsense view of what is most likely to work. Of course, if your GP is knowledgeable, he can advise you. If not, you will have to turn elsewhere.

Very often your local Citizens Advice Bureau will know what facilities are available. The appendix to this book includes the address for the Standing Conference On Drug Abuse (SCODA). They can provide a comprehensive and up-to-date list of facilities available in the UK. So, if the Citizens Advice Bureau cannot help you can contact SCODA direct.

In-patient treatment of heroin addiction is typically tackled in two parts. The first part, detoxification, which deals with the physical addiction, is generally undergone at drug clinics or the Drug Dependency Units of hospitals. In most cases a consultant psychiatrist is in charge. Again, in most cases a substitute drug such as Methodone is given in reducing amounts. The length of treatment depends on the size of the addiction.

For the second and more important part there are rehabilitation centres. They attempt to wean an addict from his psychological dependence on heroin and to help him readjust to a life without drugs. Whereas detoxification is a fairly simple, medical matter, rehabilitation is not. Different rehabilitation centres operate different programmes. Not all are equally successful and one programme may suit one type of person and not another.

Very broadly, rehabilitation centres fall into three categories, none of which is intrinsically better than the others: there are those with a Christian approach; there are concept houses based around self-help group sessions; and there are those that stress integration with the outside community. Within each category there is considerable variation in the length of treatment (which can be from three months to eighteen months), in the structure of the centre, and in its emphasis.

In theory at least, it is possible to choose between them, because, unlike drug clinics and hospitals, they do not generally operate catchment areas. In fact, the choice may be limited by the availability of places and by the attitude of your Local Authority. Your Local Authority will fund the cost of an addict's stay at a rehabilitation centre, but some will only do so if the centre is within their area. If the addict has been through a detoxification programme, the consultant psychiatrist should be able to help you with the choice, if it exists. Otherwise, there are a number of volunteer groups and advisory services that can help. One excellent source of information is the *Someone To Talk To Directory* (see Appendix).

Which rehabilitation centre is best for a particular addict depends, in large measure, on the personality of the addict. It is impossible to lay down general guidelines. However, it is worth asking centres what they estimate their success rate to be. If you do, you should also ask how they arrive at that estimation. If they merely assume that, unless they hear to the contrary, every addict remains drug-free after leaving the centre, their figures are, at best, suspect. If, on the other hand, their figures are based on follow-up research, it indicates that the figures are fairly accurate and that the centre has a serious, long-term approach to rehabilitation.

The great advantage of in-patient treatment is that the addict is removed from the drug environment, and does not have to cope with the pressure of temptation. Unfortunately, both Drug Dependency Units and rehabilitation centres tend to have waiting lists, which may extend up to three months. There may not even be a Drug Dependency Unit in your area. If there is one, it may be possible to attend as an out-patient, but again there may be a waiting list. Some even think that an addict should be kept waiting for treatment to prove that he has the motivation to stop. Should someone with a broken leg be made to wait so that he can show he really wants to be treated? What is an addict expected to do in the meanwhile?

Addiction is a daily problem. It cannot be suspended until professional help becomes available. The addict may want to stop, but feels able to do so only if he has some medicine to ease the physical withdrawal symptoms. If you can afford it, there is the private sector but clinics tend to be very expensive. Doctors who will prescribe substitute drugs to ease heroin withdrawal are generally known to the addict community, but this does not really qualify as adequate help. There appears to be no way to find out which private doctors will treat addiction and do so responsibly.

You need a solution fast, at least for the physical addiction. You want to avoid the situation in which the addict agrees to stop as soon as someone is available to treat him, but explains that meanwhile either you must support his addiction or he will be forced to steal the money. If the experts are not available when you want them, you will have to consider alternatives.

Alternatives

If no specialist doctor is available, you may be faced with the problem of obtaining the medicine to ease the withrawal symptoms. It is possible to withdraw without medicine but it is unpleasant at best. It also greatly increases the temptation to take heroin, particularly when the withdrawal is done at home, in the drug environment. There is a school of thought that withdrawal should be as unpleasant as possible so as to put the person off heroin. In my experience it puts him off addiction, not off heroin.

Now is the time to go back to your GP. Provided he is not actively unsympathetic, he may agree to help, even though he feels unqualified. If you explain that there is no qualified help available and if you are again with the addict and show that you are ready to take on responsibility for a cure and that you understand what is involved, you have a good chance of success. Then, too, there is a move to involve GPs more in the treatment of addiction by forming Community Drug Teams around them to take some of the pressure off clinics and hospitals.

There are a number of drugs that ease withdrawal. The most effective is Methodone. It is also highly addictive. It should, therefore, be prescribed only for the first four or five days, which are the worst, or at the maximum for ten days with a progressive reduction in dose from day five to day ten. There is no point losing a heroin addict to gain a Methodone addict. There are other opiate-type drugs of varying effectiveness available but none of them should be prescribed for more than ten days and some method should be found to dispense the day's dose each day. In addition, sleeping pills may be necessary for up to a month. They will need to be stronger, the weaker the opiate-type drug used.

Your GP may refuse to prescribe anything stronger than tranquillisers. These do not work during heroin withdrawal, unless one takes enough to put oneself to sleep. If the addict tells you that this is not enough, that he is going to continue taking heroin until he can get something more effective, it is worth considering a private doctor. This is better than giving the addict money with which to buy heroin. To do that is to accept that under certain circumstances heroin taking is permissible. That is not a good attitude with which to help someone give it up. If you are forced into the invidious position of having to go to a doctor who will give you whatever you ask for, it is essential first to telephone a Drug Dependency Unit. Explain the position and ask them to advise you what drug and in what quantity to ask for. As this is a telephone conversation, you can ring any Drug Dependency Unit or several if you want a consensus of opinion

I should like to stress that using a doctor who does not have a responsible attitude to addiction should be considered only in extremis. Do not accept a drug that has to be injected. Methodone, for example, is available in injectable form. It is also available in linctus, which is always to be preferred, whatever the addict tells you. Remember that you may be dealing with an addiction to the needle as well as to heroin. Addicts will sometimes crush up and inject tablets that are meant to be swallowed, an extremely dangerous practice that can be fatal.

If the addict is not undergoing an in-patient detoxification at a clinic or hospital, ideally he should withdraw from heroin away from home. If it has to be at home, he will be within reach of his heroin-taking friends. Depending on your assessment of the strength of his motivation to stop, you may feel he needs some supervision, if that is possible. This does not mean that you should be continuously mistrustful of the addict, only that you understand that withdrawal is easier, the less temptation the addict is subject to. It is vital to be aware of fluctuating willingness: however much he wants to stop, if a friend comes to see him and opens a packet of heroin under his nose, he will find it hard to resist. So it's useful if someone can be there with him to protect him and to talk to.

'I wanted to stop, I really did, and I had some Temgesic so I didn't feel too bad. All the same, the first day I came so close to scoring. I suddenly had so much empty time to fill. I couldn't concentrate on anything. I didn't feel like reading or watching the TV or anything really. In some ways I'm not sure it wouldn't have been better if I'd been feeling sick. At least that would have occupied my mind with feeling sorry for myself. Instead my mind kept turning back to smack. Just thinking about it got me so hyped up and, well, excited. So I had to ask my wife to take the next few days off work to be with me. Otherwise I'm sure I wouldn't have made it. Then at least when I got an attack of thinking about it, I could scream at her: "I want some." Then she'd remind me of all the reasons I didn't want it. It really helped. The bitch about smack is that once you start thinking about it all your good intentions and all the reasons for not taking it just go clean out of the window. It's a sort of madness, I reckon.'

Boredom, a lack of interest in anything and an inability to concentrate are typical symptoms of the early stages of withdrawal. It is a good idea to surround the addict with potentially interesting things to occupy him.

Depending on what medicine, if any, and how much of it the addict has, he may feel ill. This is best treated, in general, as if it were flu. He should be somewhere warm, although he may feel too restless to stay in bed. Hot baths and massages are very effective in relieving the aches and pains, if only temporarily. Remove as many of his worries as you can, indeed any pressure that is likely to turn his thoughts towards the escape of heroin.

In apparent contradiction to the above, you should try to persuade the addict to take exercise. The iller he feels, the less he will want to do so and, yet, the better he will feel afterwards. The extremely unpleasant restlessness of heroin illness is greatly reduced if one does something physically exhausting. And, if the exercise requires concentration, it takes one's mind off one's illness. The other reason is that excercise seems to be the primary stimulus for the production of endorphins. The sooner the addict's body starts manufacturing them again, the sooner he will feel physically well.

After withdrawal from the physical addiction, the addict has to come to terms with life without the crutch of heroin. This does not have to be done at a rehabilitation centre; it can be done at home, although again this raises the problem of the drug environment. It can, however, be argued that rehabilitation is best done in the drug environment, not in a closed drug-free community, because the addict is going to have to re-enter that environment at some point unless he is to spend the rest of his life running from heroin. However, the addict may first need some time away from the temptation of the drug environment before re-entering it.

If you wish to involve yourself with the addict's rehabilitation, the list of advisory services and volunteer groups available from SCODA can be extremely useful. They often provide not only advice but also support for both the addict and you. They also provide the opportunity for you to meet people who are going through the same thing or who have been through it and whose experience you can use. If there is not a service or group near in the list provided by SCODA, approach your Citizens Advice Bureau. The proliferation of heroin addiction and lack of facilities has spawned a mass of voluntary self-help groups not all of which are known to SCODA.

Most addicts, when they come off heroin, have little or no self-confidence. In part, this is a reaction to the removal of the chemical that gave them confidence. It is also due to the realisation that they had lost control of their lives and of the things that that loss of control made them do. Remorse is good; a lack of self-confidence is debilitating. Try then to build up an addict's confidence during rehabilitation. Most addicts are forced by necessity to be very inventive. That this inventiveness was mostly criminal is, for present purposes, irrelevant. It can equally well be applied to a legitimate, drug-free life. Stress, too, that if an addict can give up heroin, surely the problems of everyday life should seem simple by comparison. Too often these positive aspects of addiction are overlooked. Successful rehabilitation almost always depends on the addicts ability to answer the central question why? You may have to push him to answer it by asking the question. Typically, if you ask someone why he takes heroin, he will think you are an idiot and answer: 'Because I like it.' You should not be put off by this side-step. You have to go on asking why: why does he like it, why is he bored, why is he unhappy, until you arrive at the real problem. Then you can both set about trying to find some solutions. Successful rehabilitation, generally, also requires that the addict holds no secret hope of being able to take heroin again at some point in the future. Those who cannot face the idea of never being able to take heroin again are best advised to take each day at a time and consider every drug-free day a success.

There are no six easy steps to rehabilitation. There is no single right way, just as there is no single reason to explain heroin taking. Rehabilitation has to be tailored to the individual. To some extent, the closer you are to him and the better you know him, the easier this is to do.

All of the above assumes that the addict wants to, or is at least prepared to try to, stop. This may not be the case. One school of thought suggests that, if he refuses, you should wash your hands of him, that you should throw him out if he lives in your house, leave him if you live with him in his house, or never see him if you do not live with him. This is on the grounds that anything else amounts to a tacit approval, or at least acceptance, of his drug use. This may make logical sense; it makes no emotional sense, especially if the addict is your lover or spouse. Could you cope with the guilt if the next you heard of the addict was his death from an overdose in some seedy squat?

It may be that some people need drugs, either because of their personality or because they live in such hopeless social and economic conditions. This is not a decision that someone can make for themselves while taking drugs; it should be a decision and it must be taken in sobriety. You should therefore do your utmost to make the addict at least attempt a cure. If you cannot do so, you might consider the possibility of a medically supervised heroin maintenance programme. This has the advantage of putting the addict in the hands of a doctor. It also guarantees the supply and ensures that the heroin is of a known, fixed strength. However, there are only a handful of doctors able and willing to prescribe it. They are, quite rightly, very careful in choosing which patients they take on for heroin maintenance.

Maintenance is, therefore, rarely possible. You are clearly in the most difficult position if you live with the addict. If it is your house, you commit a criminal offence by allowing him to take drugs there. So, it is not unreasonable to forbid them in the house. The final alternative is to call the police. Whether he goes to prison as a result normally depends on whether he is only using the drug or supplying it as well. Some time in police custody might bring him to his senses, but a criminal record will be a disadvantage later. There is also some drug abuse in prisons. So, you should be aware of whose problem you wish to solve, yours or his.

Continuing support

To come off heroin is one thing; to stay off another. The importance of continuous support from the addict's family and friends cannot be stated too often. In some respects, it is even more important if the addict has been an in-patient at a rehabilitation centre. Readjustment to the real world after months in the safety of a closed community can be very hard.

'I came out of this rehab all ready to go. I was feeling really good and I was sure I could handle my life. I thought I'll get a job. No problem. Everything'll be fine. Well, firstly I couldn't get a job. I mean there just aren't any jobs round where I live. Then I kept running into people who were still using. At first it didn't bother me and I just thought "silly fuckers" but after a bit it started to get to me. It's easy when you're sitting in some rehab group to say how you'll handle it, but it's not the same when it's staring you in the face.'

Relapses are common. The sooner they are caught, the less damage they do. And the way to catch a relapse early is to have such a relationship with the addict that he will tell you about the relapse. Do not despair if he has a relapse. That he has given in once to the temptation does not mean that the cure has failed. Of the ex-addicts I know who have not touched heroin for more than a year, over half took it at least once more after giving it up.

What so often leads to relapses is the discrete thinking that can lead to addiction in the first place. To think, 'just this once will be all right' is so dangerous because it can be applied to each successive time. Addicts have to believe that giving up means giving up for ever. If they keep even a glimmer of hope somewhere in their mind that it will be possible to take heroin again just occasionally, that day will almost certainly arrive soon. If an addict does really believe that he can never touch it again, a relapse may seem to him a real disaster. He may have to be helped over it. Rehabilitation may have to be attempted more than once. One cannot always get it right the first time. Provided the lessons of past mistakes are learned, there is still progress.

The expression, 'once a junkie, always a junkie' is often bandied about by the ignorant. It is quite untrue, except in one respect: addiction causes a quasi-permanent body chemistry change, which can be thought of in terms of the glands learning how to stop endorphin production. There is also a considerable psychosomatic element involved: it is quite possible to think oneself into a state of heroin illness. This does not make the symptoms any the less real.

As a result, whereas it takes weeks or months to create an addiction, it takes only days to re-create one.

Sometimes addicts who give up heroin begin drinking heavily. This shows rehabilitation has not been wholly successful. To think its point is solely to help the addict to readjust to life without heroin is wrong. It should be a readjustment to life without any chemical crutches. On the other hand, alcohol is legal and relatively cheap. However, ex-addicts rarely become alcoholics because they know of something better than alcohol. In most cases, the bouts of heavy drinking last for no more than a few weeks.

There are a number of voluntary groups, such as Families Anonymous (see Appendix), that provide support for addicts after rehabilitation. They typically hold meetings at which ex-addicts can discuss their problems and get help and advice on how to stay drug-free. In addition, they provide an opportunity to make new friends who do not take drugs.

So often what keeps an ex-addict away from heroin is the realisation that life can be more fun without it.

'I took it once after stopping but not again. That once made me realise something I'd never realised before. Sure, smack takes away the pain of life. But it also takes away the real pleasure. You can't wake up in the morning on smack and see what a fantastic day it is, you can't fall in love, you can't listen to a piece of music and feel it touch you all the way up your spine. When you're on smack, you're on a plateau mid-way between the heights and the depths. That's not where I want to be.'

To find enjoyment, one very often has to look for it, and there is only one place to look. Enjoyment is a state of mind. Addicts, more than anyone, should understand this.

It is impossible to forget about heroin. There will always be times when an ex-addict is tempted to take it again. Certainly in the early stages, giving up is a 24-hour-a-day task; a relapse is a five-minute weakness. I'm still tempted but the further I move from addiction, the more I rebuild my life, the more I have to lose. I don't yet feel I can fully trust myself and that's scary. But it also makes me careful.

Glossary

This glossary is intended as an aid to understanding the quotes used in the book. It also includes most of the commonly used slang associated with heroin. However, no list can contain all such words as their popularity waxes and wanes with great rapidity.

Amp	– an ampoule. A wet amp contains clear liquid, injectable Methodone, a dry amp white, pharmaceutical heroin.
Bag	– a packet containing heroin of a fixed value, e.g. a £5 bag.
Busted	– to be arrested.
Buzz	– a pleasurable sensation or high.
Cold turkey	– the state caused by heroin deprivation to an addict.
Come off	– to give up heroin.
Cook up	– to heat heroin in water to dissolve it for injection.
Crank, crank Up	– an injection, to inject.
Crash out	– to go to sleep.
Cut	– to adulterate, for example heroin with glucose.
Dope	– a drug, specifically either heroin or cannabis.
Dry out	– to withdraw from heroin addiction.
Fix, fix up	– an injection, to inject.
G	– a gram.
Gear	– heroin.

Go down	– to be sent to prison.
Gun	– A syringe.
H	– heroin.
Habit	– an addiction.
Hit, hit up	– an injection, to inject
Hyped up	– stimulated physically.
Ill	– suffering from the symptoms of heroin deprivation.
Joint	– a cannabis cigarette.
Junk, junkie	– heroin, a heroin addict.
Nicked	– to be arrested.
Nod (out), on the nod	– to fall into, to be in, a narcotic stupor.
OD	– Overdose
Out of it	– to be strongly feeling the effects of heroin.
Pinned	– to have greatly contracted pupils as a result of taking heroin.
Rip off	– to cheat or steal.
Run	– a smuggling trip.
Scag	– heroin.
Score	– to buy a drug.
Shot, shoot up	– an injection, to inject.
Sick	– suffering from the symptoms of heroin deprivation.
Skin pop	– to inject subcutaneously.
Smack	– heroin.
Spike	– a needle of a syringe.
Stash	– to hide.
Stoned	– to be feeling the effects of heroin.
Strung out	– suffering from the effects of heroin deprivation.
Thai stick	– a type of cannabis.
Toke	– an inhalation from a cannabis cigarette.
Turn blue	– to overdose.
Works	– a syringe.

Appendix

Further information, advice and support can be sought from the following

Your family doctor

Citizens Advice Bureau

See your area directory for telephone number and address. They should be able to suggest a drug counselling agency or other local help.

Someone To Talk To Directly

Published by the Mental Health Foundation, and distributed by Routledge and Kegan Paul, this is a directory of self-help and community support agencies in the UK and Republic of Ireland. Ask at your local library, or any advice giving centre such as your Community Health Council or Citizen's Advice Bureau, for a copy where you will find a comprehensive list of support groups available.

SCODA (Standing Conference on Drug Abuse)

1-4 Hatton Place
London EC1N 8ND
This is the single most comprehensive information centre in the
UK and they can provide you with information on all hospitals,
non-statutory services, volunteer groups and projects related to
problems with drug abuse known to them.

Families Anonymous

88 Caledonian Road
London N7
01-278 8805
This is the main contact address for a chain of self-help groups, set
up by parents concerned about drug abuse, throughout the UK. To
find out if there is a group in your area, contact *Families
Anonymous* at the above address.

The Department for Health and Social Security, in conjunction
with ISDD (Institute for the Study of Drug Dependence), have
produced three booklets which are available free from:
Dept DM
DHSS Leaflets Unit
PO Box 21
Stanmore
Middlesex HA7 1AY.

These are:
What Every Parent Should Know About Drugs (DM. 1)
What Parents Can Do About Drugs (DM.2)
Drug Misuse: A Basic Briefing (DM.3)